Intimacy & Mission

Intimacy & Mission

Intentional Community as Crucible for Radical Discipleship

Luther E. Smith Jr.
Foreword by Jim Wallis

HERALD PRESS
Scottdale, Pennsylvania
Waterloo, Ontario

Library of Congress Cataloging-in-Publication Data
Smith, Luther E.
    Intimacy and mission : intentional community as crucible for
radical discipleship / Luther E. Smith, Jr.
        p.   cm.
    Includes bibliographical references.
    ISBN 0-8361-3662-4 (alk. paper)
    1. Christian communities—United States. 2. Church renewal.
I. Title.
BV4406.U6S65   1994
250—dc20   93-48790
                                                                  CIP

The paper used in this publication is recycled and meets the minimum
requirements of American National Standard for Information
Sciences—Permanence of Paper for Printed Library Materials, ANSI
Z39.48-1984.

2 3 4 5 6 7 8 9 10 03 02 01 00 99 98 97 96 95

To my sister Elaine,
Who since the beginning has been my heart's companion

Contents

Foreword

About fifteen years ago, Luther Smith came to Sojourners. Luther told us he was doing a project on intentional Christian communities. Would we be among his guinea pigs? We liked him right away, so we agreed.

Luther had lots of questions—good questions and sometimes hard ones. But he was a sympathetic questioner. And he was more than a scholar interested in communities; he was a fellow pilgrim on the road toward discipleship.

Over the years much has changed at Sojourners and the other communities Luther studied. As I read this book, I found myself smiling, laughing, and even grimacing in embarrassment at some of the things the author observed and reports about our development over the years. It was a helpful exercise for me to reflect on what has changed and what remains the same.

What has *not* changed is the central call of Jesus to radical discipleship. Sojourners remains convinced that such a commitment puts us on a path shared with brothers and sisters; that the gospel road leads us into the heart of the world's struggles and joys; and that our best companions on the journey are the poor and the oppressed, in whom we find the face of the one who called us in the first place.

What *have* changed are many of the ways and structures once chosen for our mission. Those were never supposed to be the important things. (When they become too important a community is close to its end.) The means keep changing; the ends must continue to be the focus. It might be said that key to community is doing what the old spiritual suggests: "Keep your eyes on the prize and hold on!"

Christian community is always an experiment in the gospel, much like what Gandhi called "experiments in truth." Like any experiment, community doesn't always come out the way we plan, and it is never quite completed. We're always on the way. It is critical to listen, remain flexible, adjust, keep our commitments and principles clear, and learn from our mistakes.

Sojourners is much less communal now, as well as less sectarian and less inwardly focused on our own life together. And thanks be to God, we have far fewer meetings! We are more inclusive, more open and outward looking, more balanced in our personal and corporate lifestyles, and more focused on our missions in the world. That, in my experience, is also true of other Christian communities which have survived and still flourish.

What has most changed is the context of the church. When Sojourners began in 1971, we often felt isolated in many of our concerns—sometimes like a voice crying in the wilderness. The kindred spirits we found were often in other intentional Christian communities, usually on the margins of the church. People were leaving institutional churches and joining communities like Sojourners as an alternative.

I believe Christian communities have lifted up an alternative voice and witness in both the church and the society. But today, more than two decades later, many of the commitments found in communities like Sojourners can also be found elsewhere. They are present in local congregations and parishes and more traditional religious communities. They are evident in ecumenical organizations and church bodies in virtually every denomination and all over North America. The Spirit has been working in many places, some of them quite unexpected.

I once believed that intentional Christian community would be the primary new wineskin for a transformed church. I was wrong. New forms and expressions of community are indeed essential to that transformation, but there are a myriad of models and examples. For instance, we have discovered that nearly all of *Sojourners* magazine readers are involved in a local church. More than half are part of some small community circle or group. Yet few are in residential communities.

Real community is the key, rather than any particular form of it. When I am asked if authentic Christian community can really emerge in traditional and institutional church settings, I am reminded of what Mark Twain said when asked if he believed in infant baptism. He replied, "Believe in it? Hell, I've seen it!"

Luther Smith's valuable contribution is not only profiling five communities but discerning the principles and lessons that come from those portraits. Those learnings, as the author so clearly demonstrates, are now for the whole church.

—*Jim Wallis, editor,*
Sojourners *magazine*
Washington, D.C.

Author's Preface

"If Christians would only fully commit themselves to being God's people, the church would change the world." All my life sermons, conversations, Sunday school discussions, and Christian literature have assured me that radical discipleship can transform the world. The conviction is inspiring. It suggests *the church can do something to heal a broken world*. With greater intensity and intention in commitment, the church can overcome any obstacle to realizing God's intent for creation.

As inspiring as this conviction continues to be, however, is there any evidence it is true? *Intimacy and Mission* answers this question by examining five contemporary religious communities that have mobilized the devotion and energy of believers to make visible faith's transforming power.

I confess that this question of evidence is personal. The years given to this project were energized by my hunger to know this: Are declarations about the power of discipleship just idealistic rhetoric? Or are there living testimonies to such conviction?

But the question of evidence must also be a central concern of the church itself. How else can the church assess whether it is fulfilling God's call? How else can the church be inspired and instructed by testimonies of God doing miracles through a servant people? Ever evolving are the challenges of being a Christian fellowship to meet the needs of members and society. Ever necessary is reflection upon the church's ability to keep pace with the challenges. God, who calls the church into being, also calls it into becoming.

My search for evidence not only provided insights about the meaning and possibilities of radical discipleship in religious communities, it also clarified how radical discipleship is practical for local congregations. As atypical as religious communities can seem to outsiders, they illustrate fundamental insights for the church universal. I believe, therefore, that this book will not only disclose dynamics of the studied communities but will also help members of local congregations to discern the possibilities for radical discipleship in their own lives and churches.

Chapter 1 briefly traces the ecclesiastical and historical circumstances that are the impetus for intentional religious communities. The five intentional communities which are the focus of this study are introduced. Chapter 2 presents the compelling factors that lead to the formation of the intentional communities. This chapter (and the next three) concludes with a section entitled "For the Church Today," in which the discussed insights about intentional communities are related to the ministry and mission of congregations.

Chapter 3 examines convictions about and structures of covenant that influence the quality of communal life. Attending to expectations for covenant is crucial to the vitality of religious communities. In Chapter 4, fundamental issues of authority and membership are analyzed to explain communal organization.

Chapter 5 discusses the impact of the religious communities' accomplishments and methods of social change. And Chapter 6 draws on the previous chapters to formulate perspectives that prepare and sustain radical disciples as they respond to God's call upon their lives.

My interpretation of the histories of these intentional communities has relied heavily on interviews (with community members, former members, local residents, and civic leaders) and communal documents. Over the years of research and writing, many contributed to this effort. First, I am deeply indebted to the religious communities who offered their histories and hospitality; in addition to giving many time-consuming interviews and providing access to communal archives, the communities opened to me their homes and hearts.

Special recognition goes to Phil Amerson and Robert Sabath, whose insights aided my development of the project design. Barb Tamialis, Ron Spann, Judi Jacobson, Calvin Kimbrough, Joanie Perkins, and Jophie Anderson are members of communities who gave helpful feedback on a draft of the manuscript.

The Candler School of Theology at Emory University provided academic leave, so I had extended periods of time for research and writing. The Center for Religious Research at Candler gave invaluable assistance with the computer analysis of the survey data on ninety religious communities. Staff members Jim Miller and John Medearis gave considerable time to coding data and developing the computer program. Field research and the survey of ninety communities was supported in part by a grant from the University Research Committee of Emory University.

Several Candler students assisted with various research endeavors. Their enthusiasm and support encouraged me during days when the project seemed overwhelming.

Don Shockley provided insightful comments on an early draft of the first three chapters. Helen Pearson gave invaluable feedback on several drafts and remained a dialogue partner throughout the writing. And JoAnn Stone's secretarial assistance has been steadfast.

Finally I am grateful to Michael A. King, Herald Press book editor, whose interest and encouragement were crucial to the completion of this work.

This listing of acknowledgments suggests that this book is not only about the formative power of community; it is also the result of a community of formative friends and colleagues.

—*Luther E. Smith, Jr.*
Atlanta, Georgia

Intimacy & Mission

CHAPTER 1

The Invitation to See

The Word Made Flesh

In the beginning is the image. In the image is the beginning.

Christians are a story people. Our understanding of God, creation, and ourselves relies on dramatic portrayals of our ancestors struggling to live in covenant with God. Image by image the stories are formed, and story by story new images arise that inspire (breathe life into) us and our understanding of faith.

Fundamental to the Christian story is the belief that Jesus' life reveals (images) his message and meaning. Jesus embodies his religious commitment. His life is reliable testimony for what he believes. In Jesus, the word is made flesh.

Jesus' method of revealing religious truth is also the method for his followers. As admonished in the epistle of James, Christians are to "be doers of the word, and not hearers only" (Jas. 1:22). We seek to exemplify God's will for human relationships. Our religious identity and convictions are asserted most persuasively not just in doctrine and sermons, but in the quality and character of our fellowship and outreach. The refrain of a popular Christian hymn (based on John 13:34-35 and 17:22-23) expresses this principle when it says, "They will know we are Christians by our love, by our love, yes they'll know we are Christians by our love."[1]

This Christian identity is not only defined in terms of who

we are as individuals of faith, it is also defined by who we are as a *community* of faith. Becoming Christian is more than being personally transformed; it is also participation in a transforming fellowship. Essential to Christian identity is *membership*. The Christian is a member of a fellowship of believers. This fellowship is a context where faith is imaged by its members bearing witness to its meaning and power. This fellowship is the church—a place where we expect that the word is being made flesh.

Inevitably this key question arises: When the world looks at the church, does it know the primary concerns of the Christian faith through the church's witness? On a more personal level, would a visitor to my church—after seeing how we relate to one another in our fellowship, attending a church business meeting, determining the commitments of our budget, or assessing our involvements in the society—better understand God's passion for love and justice? Most of us are reluctant to answer an unqualified "yes" to these questions.

We cry out, "Let the church be the church!" But we are perplexed about how to make the declaration a reality. This book focuses on *intentional community* as the essential model enabling the church to fulfill God's calling. Such intentionality requires churches to assess how they image the Christian faith and to do whatever is necessary to become a more vivid expression of their faith.

The institutional character of church life is often identified as the cause for the church's inability to prepare Christians to implement their faith. In both its Roman Catholic and Protestant expressions, the church has often become hierarchical and bureaucratic. The church's most active members frequently feel that their service in committees and conferences does little more than perpetuate church structures. The ultimate purpose for such structures is frequently lost in the mechanics and politics of institutional maintenance. Many laity and clergy wonder if their endless meetings on repairing and securing church properties, determining salaries, devising and revising church organizations, sending representatives to national and international church meetings, and dealing with the institution's financial problems are the primary work of the church.

Of equal importance is the criticism that the institutional church too often gives up its prophetic role in society in exchange for social acceptance. The church accommodates the values of the secular society. It develops theology and practices which endorse the materialism, nationalism, and social prejudices of the dominate culture. Often this means that the church fails to be an advocate for civil rights, the needs of the poor, justice for the oppressed, and peace between nations. To preserve the image of being a stable and affirming social institution, decisions about ministries are based on the principle that conflict must be held to a minimum, and that members should not be offended by controversial ministries.

The church is called to be a fellowship of God's servant people. Our investment in institutional maintenance must consider these questions: Have our structures and procedures deepened the discipleship commitment of members? Has our corporate life been conducted so persons feel the church is a place of healing for brokenness in their personal lives and relationships? Has the church's decision making empowered it to be a force for justice and reconciliation in the world?

Constant vigilance over the continuing institutionalization of church life is required. Otherwise our involvement in the church may sustain it as an institution and make the church a refuge from social crises—but we will fail to seek first God's realm.

Recognizing that an institutional agenda can be antithetical to the ministry of Jesus, some Christians work to reform the institutional church. They believe complex church structures can provide settings for intimate caring and bring about substantial social change. The Holy Spirit has not abandoned the institutional church but seeks to work through individuals and structures open to the Spirit's transforming power. Needed, such Christians argue, is more extensive involvement in institutional decision making by Christians with a vision for pastoral and prophetic ministries.

Other Christians believe reformation of the institutional church is either not possible or not the most effective use of their time and commitment. The church need not take institutional forms, they argue. Examining the Christian heritage, they note that—

1. Christianity started as a religious movement; the evolution into its institutional expressions is neither a biblical nor theological mandate;

2. The early Christian fellowships of the New Testament were small groups where religious instruction, discipline, and mutual care were conducted. The development of large assemblies was not perceived as a necessary goal for the fulfillment of their mission; and

3. The first Christians had no motivation to blend into their culture. The compromises that allow the church to be a popular institution undermine Christian identity, the church's critical relationship to culture, and proclamation of the gospel. Instead of resuscitating the institutional church, these Christians believe the forms and spirit of the early churches should be recaptured.[2] They therefore form new religious fellowships to avoid the pitfalls of becoming or maintaining the institutional church.

Thousands of these religious communities exist in the United States alone. A variety of terms label them—alternative churches, intentional communities, base churches, house churches, religious communities. (Note: throughout this writing these terms are used interchangeably in discussing religious communalism. The term *community* usually refers to intentional religious fellowships; however, when community is used to define *location* or *the spirit of cooperation*, the context of its use makes these meanings clear.)

These religious communities intend to create a fellowship and mission nearly as radical as the gospel they proclaim. Nearly all these communities identify themselves as a vital expression of Christ's church. Some have organized to be a haven from the turbulent world; they offer members a place secured from the issues and politics of society.

The communities on which this study focuses, however, are committed to the transformation of society. They seek to change North American life to reflect their biblical understanding of justice and compassion. This commitment is integral to their understanding of Jesus' ministry and the mission of the church.

This book will expose readers to the inner life of selected religious communities. Explored will be the communities' sense of

calling, how they are structured, crucial dynamics of membership, and the forces which sustain and threaten their existence.
We can then determine whether these communities are merely
curious experiments that make for an interesting investigation,
or a witness with the potential to alter the religious and social
landscape.

Noting the positives of religious communalism should not be
interpreted as a vote against the institutional church. To affirm
one while negating the other would pit the church against itself.
This book, therefore, is really an investigation of practical efforts
to renew the local church. There are invaluable lessons institutional churches can learn from religious communities. *But this
does not mean that local churches are to become religious communities.*
Such a conclusion would be unrealistic or undesirable for most
churches.

However, church leaders could tailor aspects of religious
communalism to fit the character and needs of their congregations. The institutional church might adopt or adapt these communities' principles of membership formation, their structuring
of decision making, their process of creating an intentional fellowship, their means of making pastoral care a corporate activity, or any number of other distinctive features which enable
communities to be nurturing and prophetic fellowships.

That religious communities are a resource to congregations
is already acknowledged by a large denomination. The United
Methodist Church, in a section of its *Book of Discipline* entitled
"The Nurturing Community," officially recommends the following to its membership.

> We . . . recognize the movement to find new patterns of
> Christian nurturing communities such as Koinonia Farms,
> certain monastic and other religious orders, and some
> types of corporate church life. We urge the church to seek
> ways of understanding the needs and concerns of such
> Christian groups and to find ways of ministering to them
> and through them.[3]

The recommendation indicates that the commitment to reform

the institutional church and the commitment to form an alternative religious community are mutually beneficial. The institutional church has traditions and resources that can increase the influence and stability of religious communities. And communities have innovative methods of fellowship and mission that can help reform the institutional church.

Intimacy and Mission tells the story of Christian disciples who are dissatisfied with any traditions and forms of organization that do not empower them to respond fully to God's call. But rather than just criticize the church, these Christians labor to establish a religious fellowship that honors God's call to radical discipleship. *Radical disciples make their devotion to God the priority which shapes all other decisions.* They labor for a fellowship of *intimacy*, where members nurture and care for one another's physical, emotional, and spiritual needs. And they work toward a fellowship of *mission*, where compassion for God's people involves the fellowship in social transformation. The testimony of these religious communities is a resource for the church as it seeks to be a vital image of the word made flesh.

The New Eden

U.S. history is replete with groups committed to creating a social reality conformed to their particular religious vision. This desire can be traced from Puritan efforts to establish a theocracy to the politics of Jerry Falwell's Moral Majority and the religious right movement which continues in its wake. Such commitment and desire have been an abiding influence upon U.S. life.

Perry Miller writes about the need to interpret Puritan settlements in America as political entities that reflected religious convictions. Responsibility for the social order was a religious calling.

> For the Puritan mind it was not possible to segregate a man's spiritual life from his communal life. Massachusetts was settled for religious reasons, but as John Winthrop announced, religious reasons included "a due forme of Government both ciuill and ecclesiasticall," and the civil was quite as important in his eyes as the ecclesiastical.[4]

The Puritans sought to establish an environment conducive to nurture of "the saints" (true Christian believers). Laws were made, governments established, and religious principles taught so community members might live the life of salvation God ordained. It is crucial to recognize, however, that the formation of religious community was conceived as a sacred mission that transcended the lives of the immediate members of the community. The Puritans saw themselves as establishing a model of God's design for the social order.

John Winthrop's sermon to his fellow passengers aboard the *Arbella* in 1630, as they crossed the Atlantic from Europe to New England, provides a penetrating insight into this sense of mission.

> . . . for we must consider that we shall be as a city upon a hill, the eyes of all people are upon us; so that if we shall deal falsely with our God in his work we have undertaken and so cause him to withdraw his present help from us, we shall be made a story and a by-word through the world, we shall open the mouths of enemies to speak evil of the ways of God and all professors for God's sake.[5]

Winthrop's message epitomizes the Puritan sense of fulfilling a divine calling to manifest God's will. They sought to form a redemptive community; that is, one which would instruct the world about God's ways.

Several purposes were at work in this mission. First, there was the effort to perfect the lives of the community's members and to foster belief and govern behavior so each member's life satisfied the requirements of the divine call. Second, the community labored to exemplify God's design for humanity. Becoming a model society would demonstrate to the world how to be the obedient people of God. Third, the society was to be a testimony to the glory of God. Forming such a society was not only a key to perfecting self and others, it was in itself an act of praise.

The impulse to form a redemptive community persisted beyond the colonial period and is clearly evident in the explosive birth of nineteenth-century communities. During that century, hundreds of communities (both religious and secular) sought to create environments that could reform society's ills. The sheer number of these groups led Ralph Waldo Emerson to write, "We are all a little wild here with numberless projects of social reform. Not a reading man but has a draft of a new community in his waistcoat pocket."[6]

This communal impulse was not fueled solely by religious motivations. Another major influence was the optimistic character of the American people. When faced with distressing circumstances, they continued to feel they had options. They believed some method, activity, or technology would remedy whatever problem confronted them.[7] The establishment of a new society always seemed within reach. It might require moral renewal, strict codes of behavior, authoritarian leadership, a redefinition of marriage and the family, or any number of innovations. But Americans were sure there were ways to establish a more advanced social order.

This sense of option and optimism was partly shaped by the process of settlement in this country. The newcomers left in Europe those political, social, and religious constraints which smothered their dreams. The transatlantic voyage was an exercise of freedom: freedom to enter a future where enforcers of the old order could not go. Etched in the American psyche was the association of this country with unlimited opportunity.

The frontier reinforced the sentiment of possibility. Here was an abundance of land that seemingly continued forever. This meant one could move elsewhere (begin anew) if the present location failed to support one's goals. Land encouraged mobility, and mobility promised opportunity.[8]

Besides the influence of land, the sense of option was also stirred by intellectual forces from Europe. The experimental methods of the enlightenment were increasingly embraced as valid means to determine truth. Such methods challenged traditional religious and secular sources of authority. Available to the "common person" was a process to discern truth through reasoning and trial. No longer bound by blind allegiance to authority, individuals were free to test untried social and religious ideals which might prove to be the solution to humanity's ills.

All these factors of optimism contributed to shaping religious visions that had ambitious plans for humanity. America represented more than an opportunity for a particular people; it existed to serve a purpose of universal proportions. A righteous nation would redeem a fallen world. Church historian Sydney E. Ahlstrom describes this outlook: "In many minds the American was conceived as a new Adam in a new Eden, and the American nation as mankind's great second chance."[9] Seeing this opportunity to correct misguided developments in church and culture, religious communities sought to take full advantage of this "second chance." With zeal Christians endeavored to establish a visible example of the kingdom of God.

Although optimism and experimentation are prevalent themes in American history, the social engineering plans of religious communities have not always been enthusiastically welcomed. The larger society, more often than not, has cast suspicious eyes upon communal groups. The history of communalism is replete with persecution, ostracism, and distrust. The tyrannical leadership of Eric Janson at the Bishop Hill colony, the complex marriage arrangements at Oneida, Father Divine's claim to be God, and the mass suicides/murders caused by Jim Jones in Guyana and David Koresh in Waco, Texas, are cases that show the potential for communalism to breed aberrant and dangerous behavior.

To select and isolate such examples is a grave injustice to religious communities whose witness has breathed life into precious social and religious principles. Ignored is the racial equality and compassionate care of the widows, orphans, and poor to be found among the Shakers. Ignored is the economic cooperation of the Amana Colonies. Ignored is the Bruderhofs' unyielding commitment to pacifism. Ignored is the genuine and profound sense of reform which exhibits Christian commitment and America's social conscience at their best.

When a comprehensive examination is made, many religious communities are found to be important creations that seek to be living testimonials to our social and religious ideals. Often they fail in their efforts. Sometimes they succeed. Regardless of failure or success, they persist. And in persisting they offer hope that faith's transforming power to establish a moral order can be seen in their fellowship and the results of their labors.

South of Eden

Within the last generation there has been a surge of excitement and expectation about the ability of Christian communities to instigate social change. Ironically, the source of this heightened enthusiasm is outside the borders of the New Eden. Throughout Latin America about 200,000 Christian communities have been created in recent decades. These communities are credited with causing profound church and social reform in their countries. They have inspired Christians in Africa, Asia, Europe, and North America to believe again in the value and power of the small Christian fellowship.

These Latin American communities are known as *communidades eclesiales de base*—translated as basic Christian communities (BCC). The term often used for these religious groups is abbreviated to "base communities." The word *basic* (or base) means popular, of the people, grassroots. The word *community* implies the sense of solidarity, mutual support, and communal identity felt by group members.

The BCCs began in the early 1960s as an effort by the Roman Catholic Church to reach millions of parishioners the church was not adequately serving. Some large parishes had only one priest for an area with 40,000 communicants. The church had directed its clerical energies to the cities, where the concentration of people (especially affluent supporters) seemed to justify the deployment of limited staff.

The dearth of pastoral leadership meant that the rural poor, those least capable of contributing to the financial needs of the church and the most difficult to reach, were becoming more alienated from the life of the church. The Catholic hierarchy organized to prepare the laity to take increasing responsibility for pastoral needs. Groups were formed with small (around ten) and large (about 150) memberships. Lay leaders were trained to lead religious communities in devotions, offer religious instruction, and help members meet one another's needs.[10]

When the laity of these communities studied the Scripture, many for the first time began relating biblical concepts of justice and love to their social context. Consequently, they developed biblical images for the social order that challenged the political, economic, religious, and social circumstances under which they presently lived. A new political consciousness and sense of religious identity emerged that critically analyzed government policy and the church's mission.

Several major outcomes have resulted from the BCCs movement. First, a legion of new leaders has been developed for influencing the future of the church and society. These laity have not replaced the priestly leadership, but have expanded the pool of leaders to which the people have access. Now the masses, especially the rural poor, have indigenous leadership who can hear their concerns and organize the people to meet crucial needs.

Second, the movement has contributed to the revitalization of the Latin American church. The reinvolvement of millions of communicants, the expansion of the church's leadership, the creative model of mutual care, the rich devotional life reflected in the hymns and prayers of the people, and the integral role of the church in some social policies have spurred growth and spiritual commitment within the church.

Third, the movement has been instrumental in forming and testing liberation theology, in which God is understood to be on the side of the poor in their struggle against oppression. In such theology the poor and oppressed are also considered sources of revelation of what God is doing in the world. Their thirst for justice is indicative of God's thirst for justice. The spread of liberation theology has caused many in the church to rethink theological formulations and mission strategies which have neglected or denigrated the poor. It has also reawakened many to the church's prophetic role of critical political analysis and action.

Fourth, BCCs have questioned and influenced government policies. The extent to which this has occurred depends on the political climate of the country in which the BCCs exist. Philip Berryman comments that the more repressive a country, the more subversive its BCCs. One can then understand why base communities suffered persecution in Nicaragua under the Somoza regime and in El Salvador.

In less repressive countries the base communities, Berryman notes, "may well be church-centered, focusing on biblical formation, regularizing common-law marriages and improving family life." But even in these political contexts the emphasis of BCCs is not totally outside the public domain. Group members may be involved in "development projects, clinics, agriculture courses or cooperatives."[11] Whether revolutionary or developmental, the base communities contribute to the social improvement of those who suffer political and economic oppression.

As stated earlier, the impact of BCCs is far reaching. In the search for models of religious community that take seriously the social mission of the church, the base communities are persuasive paradigms. This has led Harvey Cox, a noted theologian and social analyst, to conclude that

> the emergence of these new forms of church life at the local level, first in Latin America and then elsewhere, constitutes a change in the Catholic Church that may be even more influential than the Vatican Council in shaping the future of Christianity.[12]

The influence of BCCs has also affected Protestantism in the United States. Some Protestants focus on the evangelization impetus within BCCs. They see an effective model for bringing people into a vital Christian fellowship of caring and discipleship. Hopes for church growth are raised by BCCs. Others are drawn to the church renewal impetus. They find in BCCs a model for lay led worship and church programs. The break from hierarchical and bureaucratic church organization provides a new wineskin for the outpouring of new wine (the Holy Spirit).

The BCCs' social transformation impetus appeals to those who long to see the church address social issues that threaten life. Base communities offer an example of the logic and possibility of Christian love in the political realm where the church has often seemed anemic or impotent.

Caution, however, must be taken in transferring the BCC

model to the United States. Substantial cultural differences exist between the two contexts, making a blanket cross-cultural application of base communities inappropriate. The religious difference is most obvious. Catholicism is the dominant expression of Christianity in Latin America. With it comes a revered tradition of church practices and religious authority that have shaped the history and culture of that region. The Catholic Church has a definite structure of authority that can articulate the church's position on issues. While differences exist within the Catholic Church, a Latin government is not confused over who officially represents the church's voice in the society.

In the United States Protestantism is the major religious expression. Consequently, the diverse Christian traditions and understandings of religious authority completely alter the scenario of church influence. In this nation of religious pluralism there are myriad religious voices, all claiming to be official for multitudes of people.

The socioeconomic differences between Latin America and the United States also limit the application of the base communities model. Economically, most of Latin America is underdeveloped, while the U.S. is a developed country. A movement such as the BCCs which focuses upon the poor is addressing the needs of the masses. Poverty is so pervasive and has been the socioeconomic reality for so long that the poor are not censured for their plight.

In the United States, on the other hand, the poor are a minority whose condition is often interpreted as indicating moral defect or laziness in a land of opportunity. When the base communities concept has been used by Christian fellowships in the U.S., the enthusiasm for evangelization, church renewal, and social transformation has not always included the poor and oppressed. Often such middle-class fellowships only aim to spread the gospel to other middle-class folk. They seek to deepen the involvement of middle class laity in the church. If there has been any social commitment, such issues as nuclear disarmament, abortion, and the environment have filled the political agenda.

The theological emphasis of BCCs contains a socioeconomic

analysis that prevents unqualified adoption of the BCCs model. The liberation theology which nourishes the BCCs relies heavily on a Marxist critique of society. Marxism's stress on the inevitability of class conflict and its condemnation of capitalism is an extremely unpopular analysis in the U.S. Those advocating such a view are often labeled as courting communism. And since communism is judged incompatible with democracy, the patriotism of those entertaining a Marxist critique is questioned. In addition, the collapse of communism in Eastern Europe is considered evidence by many that communism is a failed system.

Some black U.S. scholars have also been at odds with the Marxist critique. They believe that while Marxism may be helpful in identifying issues related to poverty, it fails to assess the noneconomic dimensions of racism. The oppression of black Americans will not be relieved unless there is a thorough analysis of the psychology, politics, and theology of racism. Because it fails to grapple with racism as a major social and religious issue, the liberation theology of the BCCs needs revision before it adequately interprets U.S. realities.[13]

Despite these cultural differences, the BCCs serve as inspiring examples of religious communities' ability to answer God's call to radical obedience. The rich devotional life, the sustaining of caring fellowships, and the prophetic witness to structures of injustice are marks of this obedience. And since the church universal is called to the same obedience, the base communities are encouraging signs that faithfulness to such a demanding call is possible. So while BCCs are not blueprints for application to every cultural context, they are testimonies of ministry and mission that have bearing on all contexts. Justice, the nurturing of caring fellowships, and the preparation of Christian disciples are the work of the church everywhere. Base communities, as the body of Christ, reveal how the word can be made flesh. And in so doing they comply with the urge to *see* an example of faith incarnate.

The need remains, however, to experience the vital expression of faith in one's own situation. The effort to provide such a vital expression in the United States through the development of religious communities has proceeded on an extraordinary scale.

Thousands of religious communities have been organized as fellowships of worship, mutual care, and mission. And although the BCCs movement inspires many of these communities, their identity is primarily forged by the traditions and challenges encountered in the U.S.

Modern Testaments

The search to find, understand, and derive treasures of meaning from religious communities is exciting. The adventure not only tests skills of discernment, it challenges the very depths of our commitment. After encountering the faith lived in these communities, one is never the same.

This book will hopefully contribute to a deeper understanding of the community movement but cannot claim to fully analyze such a complex topic. This exploration of communities is therefore limited to communities which meet several criteria.

First, the community is *intentional* about shaping the structures and directions of its existence. The community has not simply inherited procedures, structures, and a tradition of group interaction it feels compelled to continue. The members of the community are the architects of communal life and mission.

Second, community membership is characterized by an intense commitment to sustaining, *on a daily basis*, a Christian fellowship where members share time, resources, and labors to further the community's mission. Members are also committed to living in the locations of the people they serve; theirs is a ministry of presence with the poor and oppressed.

Third, the community professes it is called by God to be a *prophetic witness* against social injustice. Members not only pray for positive change in the social order, they interact with social systems to affect a more just society.

Fourth, the behavior of members falls within *normative patterns of Christian conduct*. The mention of communal life often conjures images of people engaged in multiple sexual relations, or of cults where charismatic leaders control the will and activity of members, or of groups which so reject the modern era that recent technologies and social institutions are spurned. Most

Christians feel such communities have little to offer the church in its search for models. This research has therefore carefully avoided drawing data from such communities.

Fifth, the community *has a history*. It has existed over sufficient time to assess its merits. Only after a community has endured for some years can the wisdom of internal structures or the effectiveness of mission projects be determined.

Selected for investigation are five communities that meet the above criteria. Together they yield important insights about the procedures and promise of Christian communities. They certainly do not exhaust all the possibilities of Christian community, but within their stories are dynamics experienced in many other communities that match the five criteria. This is not an effort to write the history of these communities, but to analyze it. Through such analysis we gain more sensitive understanding of the communities. More important, we come to appreciate what they can teach the larger church about Christian discipleship.

Koinonia Partners

One of the oldest communities existing today, Koinonia began in 1942 under the leadership of biblical scholar Clarence Jordan. For over half a century Koinonia has inspired Christians with its efforts "to be a demonstration plot of what Jesus meant by the Kingdom of God."[14]

Located outside Americus, Georgia, Koinonia members have farmed and lived simply so the poor and oppressed might benefit from their labors. The desire to strengthen the sense of interdependence within their fellowship, the goal of modest living, and their limited resources led members to live together in households.

They also instituted the economic requirement that individuals joining Koinonia relinquish any claim to personal financial assets and participate in Koinonia's common treasury. Under the common treasury arrangement the total community decided the needs and financial allowances for each member. Members believed that living communally demonstrated a commitment to be a Christian fellowship where cooperation and service outweighed personal ambitions and the accumulation of wealth. In this way Koinonia sought to emulate the commitment and practices of the New Testament church.

Koinonia believed that care for neighbors was as important as energies given to developing a supportive fellowship. The community successfully initiated efforts to improve the productivity of neighbors' farming and marketing methods. Koinonia shared extra food, provided emergency loans, and was a caring presence to neighbors in times of need. The community also sponsored educational and cultural programs for the youth of their vicinity.

In spite of this charitable spirit, this rural Christian community has had a turbulent history that bears the scars of discipleship. During the 1950s Koinonia was the target of numerous violent attacks because its members were in fellowship with black people. Locally the community was treated as a pariah. Merchants refused to conduct business with the farm, property was destroyed, members lived in the shadow of death, and churches rejected Koinonians for membership.

But tremendous national support flowed from persons who believed in the principles for which Koinonia existed. These persons contributed money, petitioned President Dwight Eisenhower to protect the community, helped Koinonia to cope with the local boycott of its produce, and created a national awareness about the mission and perils of Koinonia. Throughout this dangerous time Koinonia remained committed to interracial fellowship and nonviolence.

However, not long after the violence ceased in the early 1960s, Koinonia's members began to leave for various reasons. Some were dissatisfied with life at Koinonia, while others were attracted to new challenges away from the community. Although the farm had grown from 440 to 1100 acres, by 1968 only two couples remained.

Considerable effort went into rethinking the organization and mission of the community. This resulted in the 1970 restructuring of the community and the changing of the community's name from Koinonia Farms to Koinonia Partners. Though some organizational dynamics changed, Koinonia remained a residential community that lived simply, practiced economic sharing, and fostered a nurturing fellowship (members of this group are called Resident Partners).

The new mission called for Koinonia to be more ambitious in developing programs to aggressively attack problems that wreak havoc on the lives of the poor. Funding for this mission primarily came from a mail order business (established in the 1950s) that sold pecans, fruitcakes, and candies. Also marketed were books and taped messages by Clarence Jordan (who had died in 1969), and other literature that reflected the values of the community.

This profitable business has enabled the community to build over 180 houses for the poor, create a paralegal services program for the indigent, establish a neighborhood grocery store, support efforts to improve the quality of education in the local public schools, offer a summer enrichment program for youth, and develop employment opportunities for neighbors.[15] Its approach in housing engendered the creation of "Habitat for Humanity," which has an outstanding reputation for building houses for the poor throughout the world.

The restructuring of Koinonia also involved the creation of a board of directors that recommends and evaluates programs and decides how the business should develop. This board is predominantly composed of persons who do not live at the farm. This is Koinonia's way of inviting involvement that does not require communal living.

Such adjustments have aided the growth and impact of the community. In 1993, with fifteen Resident Partners, the community had membership stability, and its social witness continued to be an impressive labor of Christian love.

Koinonia's history provides the opportunity to discover how a religious community can prevail over traumatic onslaughts of change. Within Koinonia's story one may find answers to this problem which has caused the demise of most religious communities.

Sojourners
Sojourners is probably the most renowned religious community in the U.S. Through publication of its magazine, which has had

over 50,000 subscribers, this community has profoundly influenced the country's social and religious conscience. Providing religious commentary upon social issues has characterized the community's thrust since its inception in 1971.

The community's first publication, *Post American*, proclaimed America's Vietnam War policies to be morally and spiritually bankrupt. Since then the magazine (now called *Sojourners*) has continued to be a prophetic publication, providing a Christian interpretation of controversial domestic and international issues.

The seminarians who founded Sojourners (originally called the Peoples Christian Coalition) soon decided that in addition to their journalistic task they were called to be a religious community. They structured a communal form of life within a low-income Chicago neighborhood. However, by 1974 internal disagreements led to the termination of the communal experiment.

After a period of soul-searching on the meaning of community, a few of those who had stayed together decided to try becoming a community again. The increasing affluence of their neighborhood caused them to search for a new place to establish their fellowship and to serve. In 1975 they relocated to an impoverished black neighborhood of Washington, D.C.

Sojourners began to expand rapidly. The popularity of its magazine and the hunger of persons searching for a communal experience considerably increased its membership. In 1976 there were fifteen members; by 1980 there were fifty. Members lived in extended households; these were living situations in which several different families occupied a house.

Members were also expected to relinquish or give to the community all of their financial assets upon joining. Even those who continued to work in jobs outside the community would turn over their paychecks to the community. Members would then have their living expenses determined and receive an allowance from Sojourners' common treasury. Such living and economic arrangements helped forge the sense of identity and the spirit of cooperation that have given birth to Sojourners' ministries.

The intense fellowship also generated conflicts that threatened the stability of the growing community. A membership process was devised to help persons know the realities of communal life before joining. An extensive orientation period prepared candidates to live communally and sensitized them to Sojourners' mission commitments. In addition to the magazine, the community has fought to provide affordable housing for low income neighbors, organized poor tenants into a union that protested unjust housing policies and practices, operated a day-care program, provided emergency food and shelter for the needy as well as an enrichment program for local youth, organized national demonstrations to protest the country's military and foreign policy decisions, and published literature that extols Christian communalism and social transformation. Through its lifestyle and various ministries, Sojourners has sought to bear witness to the Christian ideals of peace, justice, and identification with the poor and oppressed.

About 1988, internal dissatisfaction with communal life and the demoralizing feeling that prevailed because no new members had joined in three years led to dramatic changes at Sojourners. The common treasury and common household living arrangements were discontinued as features of the fellowship. Still most members continued to question if the community fulfilled their sense of calling. Within a brief period, the community went from thirty to thirteen members. In 1992 Sojourners had twelve adult members, but the community felt a strong sense of cohesiveness and a renewed enthusiasm for their life together.

When intensely committed persons come together to establish a common witness, they have surges of unity countered by competing agendas and factions. Sojourners' story contains fascinating insights on the enormous potential and complexity of prophetic communities.

Church of the Messiah
In the 1920s Messiah was one of the largest Episcopal parishes in Michigan. By 1971 it was gasping for life. The changes of its inner-city Detroit neighborhood and the attendant drift of members to other suburban churches had stripped the church of support. Faced with bleak prospects, new leadership was brought to

the church in hopes of sustaining its ministry.

Three dramatic changes occurred in 1971 which stimulated the rebirth of Messiah. First, the hiring of a black priest (Ron Spann) helped the predominantly white congregation become relevant to its increasing black neighborhood.

Second, the leadership introduced charismatic devotion that enlivened worship and deepened the membership's spiritual growth. This attracted new members.

Third, many members felt their new spiritual commitment could be nurtured best in a communal environment where caring for one another and praise of God were primary. The church was therefore reorganized so some members could function as a religious community (later called Common Life).

In forming its communal life, Messiah maintained the option for persons to be church members without joining the religious community. The church was bound by the membership rules of the Episcopal Church; membership therefore had to be extended to anyone who expressed a desire to join the parish.

However, participation in Common Life, with its extended household arrangements and common treasury, was increasingly understood to be the mark of committed membership. This meant living in the neighborhood of the church, being involved in the various activities of the Common Life group, simple living, and the necessity to relinquish financial assets upon joining the group. By 1978, about 100 of Messiah's 170 members participated in Common Life. Messiah grew from a church struggling for survival to a burgeoning charismatic community.

But Messiah took another unusual step which most charismatic fellowships avoid; it became involved in social concerns by addressing peace and justice issues. With its elementary school, housing corporation, service to nursing homes, classes for the mentally disabled, participation in neighborhood organizing, and public demonstrations against militarism, Messiah invested financial resources and physical energies in social needs as a vital expression of its communal identity.

This prophetic step, however, was enacted at a price to communal harmony. The greater Messiah's involvement in prophetic ministries, the greater the tensions within its communal life.

Many members who joined Messiah because of its charismatic orientation and communal structure were not enthusiastic about the social and political involvements. Messiah soon experienced membership attrition. Internally, this attrition was increased by financial crises and dissatisfaction with communal structures and procedures. Externally, fear of the neighborhood and persons feeling called to other life pursuits added to membership loss. In 1985 the Common Life group had only twenty-two of Messiah's 110 members. By 1987 the Common Life group was dissolved.

A few persons continue to live in households and gather for nurture in small groups. Except for the closing of its school and daycare center in 1986, the church continues to support the various ministries. The Common Life experience, although now terminated, still has a profound and constructive effect on Messiah's continuation as a pastoral and prophetic fellowship. A study of Messiah shows the types of struggles a local church will likely face in adopting a communal structure and prophetic ministry. And Messiah, because it always cultivated its ties to its denominational hierarchy, offers a useful example of how a local church can blend communal and established church structures.

Voice of Calvary (VOC)

Voice of Calvary has a form of communal life quite different from the above communities. Especially noteworthy is the absence of extended households and common treasuries as mechanisms of group cohesion. At VOC "community" has meant to live within a particular neighborhood under a common Christian commitment to work for the neighborhood's viability.

Founded in 1975 by John Perkins, the noted African-American Christian activist, VOC has sought to empower the black community through economic development and the creation of alternative social institutions. Using the skills and energies of white Christians working cooperatively with black Christians has been a basic strategy in this ministry with the poor and oppressed.

To identify the membership of Voice of Calvary, we must consider two entities that are related yet distinct. There is the

Voice of Calvary Ministries (VOCM) that John Perkins created to be a model for training Christians about effective approaches to neighborhood development. Some of the personnel are permanent staff who direct its various programs. VOCM also depends upon longterm (one-five years) volunteers sponsored by their local churches or other funding sources to assist the work of VOC Ministries. These volunteers have been required to raise at least 80 percent of their salary before coming to VOCM.

As more volunteers have come from the local neighborhood and eventually become staff, their wages have become part of the VOCM budget. The salary scales are relatively low so staff can better identify with the economic limitations which the poor experience. How they live within that income is their responsibility. They may become secretaries, bookkeepers, financial development specialists, computer programmers, or fill other positions related to the administration and programs of the VOCM organization.

Although VOCM requests volunteers with specific skills, it is willing to accept and retrain persons who come without needed abilities but with a commitment to serve. VOC Ministry in Jackson, Mississippi, has focused on housing development, establishing economic cooperatives, creating educational programs that supplement the work of the public schools, and providing health care.

VOCM influence, however, spreads far beyond Jackson. Inspired by the courageous activism and charisma of John Perkins, persons come to VOCM to be trained in community development techniques. VOCM conducts a ten-week summer internship for about twenty college students. High school age youth from churches come by busloads for training and volunteer work for one or two weeks. And many other neighborhood awareness programs are designed for church groups and individuals. This attests to the substantial role which VOCM has played in training hundreds of people in theological doctrine and practical methods that empower Christian involvement in neighborhood development. VOCM's impact has reached across the U.S. and into countries of Africa and the Caribbean.

In addition to VOC Ministries, there is the Voice of Calvary

Fellowship (VOCF), organized as a local church. Initially, the Fellowship served as a chapel to the Ministries, but then it took on a full life of its own. The Fellowship sought to create a worship life and church programs that would appeal to local residents. It became the primary context for nurturing the spiritual and group life of VOC Ministries personnel.

For most of its life VOC has operated with these two bodies of members. Even though most of the Ministries' staff participated in the life of the Fellowship, it was not until 1986 that VOCM personnel were required to join the VOCF. This policy change sought to unify the thrusts of the two organizations. However, the requirement for membership was not reciprocal. In fact, many of the local residents who were part of the Fellowship were not fully acquainted with the operations of the Ministries. Whether VOC is able to develop a single membership identity out of two bodies with such different emphases and structures is yet to be seen.

In 1992 VOCF had about 225 members. This number was slightly down from a growth period in the early 1980s. VOCM had twenty-six paid personnel in 1992. VOCM struggled with a financial crisis that threatened the stability of its programs. VOCF had membership stability but felt requirements for high commitment were inhibiting its ability to attract new members.

Noteworthy is that VOC members consider themselves evangelical Christians. Adherents to evangelical Christianity believe all moral truth comes from biblical principles. Living a life of personal piety is also stressed. And they tend to embrace conservative theological and political doctrines. While John Perkins' theology follows this description, he breaks with most evangelicals by declaring that such an orientation also mandates involvement in the liberation of the poor and oppressed. Perkins has persuaded many evangelical Christians that their social conservatism is heretical.

VOC seeks to channel this conviction into a commitment to and skills in economic development for the poor. This reforming of the evangelical social agenda is an unusual process that merits examination. Voice of Calvary also provides the opportunity to see how the concept of community is shaped under black leadership focused on the economic development of black people.

Patchwork Central

Although it has been the smallest of the selected communities, Patchwork Central has a sophisticated approach for systemic change. Patchwork, like VOC, never instituted the common treasury or extended household. It rejected intensive living arrangements for fear they would absorb energies needed for mission. Still Patchwork's form of community calls for considerable commitment to intensive caring relationships with others and empowering the poor of their neighborhood.

In 1977 the six founding members of Patchwork began their ministry together in Evansville, Indiana. Patchwork members signed a yearly covenant in which they agreed to

1. practice the disciplines of prayer, worship, study, and transformation of oppressive institutions;

2. educate their children in Christian values and "encourage in them such virtues as justice, love, nonviolence, imagination, and trust";

3. live simply and devote a portion of their incomes to Patchwork's ministries;

4. work toward achieving a specific mission goal that utilizes the members' particular gifts;

5. become deeply involved in the personal growth of one another; and

6. take responsibility for the organization, program development, and administration of the community.

While not a requirement of the Statement of Covenant, it was also expected that covenant members live in the neighborhood of the community's ministries. The members committed themselves to earn wages in ministries that would contribute to the welfare of their city. The six founding members worked in the areas of counseling, teaching, campus ministry, local television, parish ministry, and daycare for children.

Initially they agreed to give at least 3 percent of their incomes to their corporate ministry at Patchwork. This designated figure was changed within three years to a statement which read, "We are committed to sharing our incomes at levels which reflect our commitment to each other and to the mission of Christ through Patchwork." The modification suggests that the community did not feel the need to identify a figure of economic commitment. To focus on the financial contribution of each member would distort the true picture of the members' sacrifice for their intentional community. They earned modest wages in their jobs, and their commitment to simplicity helped them to meet family and Patchwork needs.

But the contribution which gave birth to a closer involvement in one another's lives and to mission was time. Each member gave enormous amounts of time to assisting other members with projects related to their jobs and with their community sponsored ministries. New programs of social service, employment, and education resulted from these involvements.

In 1982 five of ten covenant members withdrew from the community because of dissatisfaction with the quality of communal relationships. The remaining members were distraught, for the exodus shattered illusions about the community's stability and raised questions about its future.

Recognizing that more persons were needed to direct the many programs and organization, the community redefined the criteria for membership in 1984. Living in the immediate neighborhood was no longer required, and the extensive commitments of time to ministries and group life were lessened.

Ironically, as the expectations for extensive time commitments from covenant members were reduced, the outreach ministries expanded. The new covenant resulted in an increase of members (from five to eighteen), which reinvigorated the community's work. Patchwork has continued to operate under this revised structure with about the same number of members.

Since this approach does not require the intensive living arrangements of Sojourners, Koinonia, and Messiah, it will probably attract those searching for a model to implement in their local church. Instead of identifying the community's thrust, then drafting members to staff it, this approach affirms the individual's calling, then mobilizes the community on its behalf.

Even the name "Patchwork" symbolizes the community's emphasis on the individual. It refers to the beauty and usefulness of a quilt—a single object composed of many distinctive patches. The Patchwork model should prove especially attractive to congregations wanting to establish a corporate witness to social needs while also offering support to members already involved in significant social outreach through their careers.

So while the five communities meet criteria that isolate them as a particular type of religious community, they are in no way identical. They are located in the rural and urban South, northern inner-cities, and small-town America. The memberships express theologies which are evangelical, charismatic, liberal, orthodox, and eclectic. They have different internal structures and different ministries. Though they have multiple contexts and methods, they have a single commitment to creating intimate Christian fellowship and a mission of justice.

The insights gleaned from the five communities have been compared with data from a survey of sixty-eight religious communities that share this commitment to intimacy and social change. Such a survey helps verify how the five communities truly reflect the larger phenomenon of socially committed communities. This is especially important since the five communities are Protestant, while many of the religious communities in the U.S. are Catholic. In the survey, almost half of the communities are Catholic.[16] This comparative material is primarily presented in each chapter's notes.

Religious communities symbolize hope. In them members experiment with methods that enable ideals to become reality. However, the instructive potential of religious communities may finally depend on the larger church's readiness to accept and respect them as legitimate expressions of faith in action. Prejudging communal participants as misfits from society and the institutional life of the church will probably form a bias against finding any constructive purpose in religious communalism. We must remember that truth can only be discovered if we forsake the arrogance of certainty and adopt humility for seeking.

Christians discover by searching. When we are compelled to pursue truth as it is being lived in God's world, we increasingly realize what God intends. We are a pilgrim people who ask so that what is ultimately needed might be given; who seek to find;

who knock so that doors might be opened. Religious communities are places of searching and discovery. They are places where Christians have failed and succeeded in their efforts to develop an effective church witness. They are places where failure and success are instructive and inspiring to the ongoing work of the church. They are places that provide the church methods of discipleship that renew commitment and hope.

We are so easily ensnared by cultural standards of success that we sometimes ignore or dismiss other revealing sources of discipleship. An expanding church complex with a parking lot full of cars gets our attention. The new members resulting from a church's evangelism program, or considerable sums of money collected during a stewardship campaign, convince us a church has something to teach us.

While such churches may be instructive, the work of faith is not determined by the ability to gather crowds or build church campuses or collect mammon. These things may be useful in making disciples but are not sufficient in themselves. Something more is required in forming a people who exercise radical obedience to God. And for this we need to be alert to guiding images in places never suspected as sources of revelation.

The rationale for this book is informed by a passage of Scripture that gives an account of another seeker after religious truth. When the disciple Philip found Nathanael, he proclaimed "We have found him of whom Moses in the law and also the prophets wrote, Jesus of Nazareth, the son of Joseph."

Nazareth was such a nondescript town, suggesting no promise of fostering greatness, that Nathanael questioned this discovery by asking, "Can anything good come out of Nazareth?"

Philip could have begun a long disputation on stereotypes about such towns. Or he could have taken offense at Nathanael's reluctance to share his enthusiasm. Instead, Philip simply says, "Come and see" (John 1:44-46). Philip's response is an invitation to experience the reality about which they speak. It is an invitation to go beyond discussing Jesus to being with him.

By closely examining specific communities, this study seeks to avoid the trap of a theoretical discourse on the ecclesiastical legitimacy of such groups. Neither is a philosophical discussion needed on the merits of communal formation. The religious truth of these communities is discovered in their witness. We must know their story if we are to determine how faithful they are to the gospel's radical call. Therefore the method of examination is not simply philosophical but phenomenological, focused on the actualities of particular communities. And the following pages are written as an invitation to "come and see."

CHAPTER 2

The Call to Community

To Be a Peculiar People

In 1941 Martin England, a Baptist missionary, wrote a letter professing that Jesus' teachings and life require Christians to make radical commitments. England gave an example of what such a commitment might be when he said,

> If the barriers that divide man, and cause wars, race conflict, economic competition, class struggles, labor disputes are ever to be broken down, they must be broken down in small groups of people living side by side, who plan consciously and deliberately to find a way wherein they can all contribute to the Kingdom according to their respective abilities. . . . Suppose each would commit himself fully to the principle that the strong must bear the burden of the weak (mainly by helping, teaching, and inspiring him to bear his own burdens as his strength in his fellowship grows) . . . "to each according to his need, from each according to his ability" in things material as in everything else . . . that each should trust in the spirit of God working in the group to take care of his needs in illness or old age and for his dependants [sic] . . . accepting the principle of stewardship and renouncing the anti-Christian and contradictory principle of ownership . . . accepting the princi-

ple of the obligation of the Christian to produce all he can
and to share all above his own needs.[1]

After Clarence Jordan read this proposal (which had been circu-
lated in a newsletter) he and England developed a relationship
which led to their cofounding Koinonia Farms.

England's letter contains the basic tenets of the call to community. First, there must be religious vision that is rooted in the
biblical revelation of Jesus' life and ministry. Such a vision
clarifies God's will for humanity, and it directs Christian commitment to become involved with humanity so that the kingdom
of God is foreshadowed.

Second, a fellowship that expresses the vision must be
formed. Christian faith is best nurtured and made manifest in
the context of a fellowship. A fellowship that embodies the vision also demonstrates to the world the meaning, purpose, and
power of faith.

Third, the Christian fellowship should encourage members
to care for one another and for those who are outside the community. Christians, as disciples of Jesus, must endeavor to represent his work of comforting, reconciling, and liberating the
poor and oppressed.

This call to community is usually not a burning bush encounter, but it is a reverent response to history. The "yes" for community results from the cumulative impact of lessons from one's
past. At age twelve, one of these lessons was embedded within
Clarence Jordan's heart. Soon after joining the church, he observed a chain gang warden enthusiastically singing in the choir,
"Love Lifted Me." The next night Jordan heard a cry of pain as a
convict was being tortured by this devout warden.

Jordan recalls, "That nearly tore me to pieces. I identified totally with that man in the stretcher. His agony was my agony. I
got really mad with God. If He was love and the warden was an
example of it, I didn't want anything to do with Him."[2] Jordan,
the boy, experienced an inconsistency between faith and relationships which Jordan, the man, sought to eliminate through
Koinonia.

A similar process is evident in the commitment of Sojourners founder Jim Wallis. In his autobiography, *Revive Us Again*, Wallis discloses how he became disillusioned with U.S. society and the church for their failure to assault racism and Vietnam War policy with the force of their ideals. He was driven by the need to resolve the contradiction between Christian principles and American social policy.

Wallis' pilgrimage led to the realization that the Bible, when properly interpreted, mandated the church to oppose vigorously the oppression he witnessed. The church simply needed to fulfill its prophetic calling. Wallis concluded that for himself and others who shared the vision of a prophetic church, "to talk of the church meant to talk of community."[3]

The life of John Perkins leads to community from a quite different perspective. Where Jordan and Wallis identify with those who suffer oppression, Perkins is a victim of oppression. His early life in Mississippi was marked by poverty, discrimination, and racial violence.

Perkins became frustrated with the zeal of churches to rid the world of personal sins (e.g., drinking, infidelity, and gambling) while ignoring the sins of racism and exploitation. He came to see "a fellowship of blacks and whites, rich and poor, who would live together, worship together and reach out together as the people of God" as a model which could demonstrate Christianity's power to overcome the cultural divisions that had devastated his family and race.[4]

So within the personal history of a religious community's founder, one can identify situations where faith seemed incapacitated to respond to social crises. The call to community is perceived as the opportunity to test the ability of Christianity to correct distorted images of the church's fellowship and mission.

As crucial as such life experiences can be, other factors play a major role in the decision for community. Primary are biblical and theological interpretations which point to community as a vital structure for the realization of God's purposes. The use of the term *community* to characterize these religious groups has a biblical basis. Community is a translation of the Greek word *koinonia*. Other meanings of koinonia include "sharing," "communion," or "fellowship." The word is used in Acts to describe the gathering of the early church. After Peter preached to the multitude and baptized them, many persons "devoted themselves to the apostles' teaching and *fellowship*, to the breaking of bread and the prayers" (Acts 2:42, emphasis added). The religious communities interpret the following verses as a description of what such fellowship implied:

> And fear came upon every soul; and many wonders and signs were done through the apostles. And all who believed were together and had all things in common; and they sold their possessions and goods and distributed them to all, as any had need. And day by day, attending the temple together and breaking bread in their homes, they partook of food with glad and generous hearts, praising God and having favor with all the people. And the Lord added to their number day by day those who were being saved. (Acts 2:43-47)

The communal life is the response to being new persons in the name of Jesus Christ. The early church established a method of sharing (also evident in Acts 4:32-37) which these communities perceive as a pattern for Christian discipleship. Florence Jordan, wife of Clarence Jordan, recalls that when Clarence read Acts, "He said, 'Why won't it work?' So we tried it."[5]

John Perkins indicates the influence of these Scriptures on the formation of Voice of Calvary when he says,

> Though Mississippi might not have offered any historical precedents for a reconciled fellowship, the book of Acts did. We drew inspiration particularly from the Antioch fellowship—a church which demonstrated both the possibility and the necessity of reconciliation within the Body of Christ.[6]

While Sojourners' convictions for community are also based upon biblical passages, the initial motivation to form community may have been more ideological than theological. The founders of Sojourners came together to publish a tabloid that would be a

Christian critique of U.S. social policies. The urgency of issues surrounding the Vietnam War brought cohesion to the group. Even though these seminarians were living in proximity to one another, they had not attempted to establish an intentional structure and covenant of communalism.

In time, however, members felt that the increasing sense of solidarity in mission they experienced implied they should become a Christian community. In 1972 they decided to live communally. In 1974, after bitter conflict over the shape and direction of their life together, the community was dissolved. The magazine they published was a success; their effort to be a community was a failure.

Several members continued to live in extended households. They hoped to discover what shape, if any, their fellowship together was to take. During this period of searching a few members met with Graham Pulkingham, who was rector of Church of the Redeemer in Houston, Texas. Redeemer had gained national attention for the renewal and growth it experienced as an inner-city parish. Seemingly trapped in a deteriorating location with the consequential loss of membership, Redeemer's future was bleak in 1965. However, under the leadership of Pulkingham, who was deeply involved in charismatic renewal, by 1971 the church's attendance had risen from 600 to 2200 and its financial situation was secure.

In addition to the charismatic emphasis, the new communalism of Redeemer was credited with its success. Redeemer had over 500 people participating in fifty households.[7] It is therefore obvious why Sojourners' members felt that Pulkingham could offer authoritative advice about the vitality of community. And the advice they received converted them to embrace pastoral nurturing as an essential activity of community. Mutual caring was now considered as essential as the prophetic challenge to social systems.

Redeemer also influenced the development of Church of the Messiah. Before Ron Spann began his responsibilities in 1971 as rector of Messiah, he visited Redeemer to better understand how charismatic renewal (in which he was already involved) could revitalize a congregation. His observations of Redeemer's ministry and his conversations with Pulkingham emboldened his hope for Messiah. In addition, Redeemer sent two of its members to Messiah for a year, to aid Messiah's rebirth. Messiah's conviction to use a community structure was reinforced through Redeemer's example and support.

Certainly both Sojourners and Messiah were impressed with the numerical growth and vitality at Redeemer. But Redeemer exemplified something more important than successful expansion. Redeemer was perceived to be a demonstration that Christians could structure their lives to meet the biblical demand for total commitment. The dynamic spirit of the New Testament churches seemed to thrive within the community structure of Redeemer. Redeemer offered a persuasive testimony that communal living empowered Christians to love as fully as the Bible taught.

The call to community takes a different shape among Patchwork Central's founders. Creating a community that mirrored a biblical model was not their objective. Its members sought to discover new church forms that could respond to modern demands for personal nurture and social change. In part, this seeking was a reaction to the United Methodist structure in which they were involved. The Methodist approaches to developing ministry in the local parish were so entangled in bureaucracy, financial needs, and career advancement that often the church lost focus of its real purpose.

This seeking was also to test the Patchwork dream of living under a Christian covenant that bound them to care for one another and to serve the world. They envisioned community as the form that would enable them to pursue a lifestyle of discipleship without being shackled by institutional routines. So, while Patchwork did not share in the other communities' objective of reflecting a biblical model of fellowship, its level of commitment to fulfill the commission of discipleship was just as intense.

Patchwork's more *functional* attitude toward communalism resides, to some degree, within all the selected communities. A communal structure has practical advantages not dependent on a religious rationale. A limited membership size, the interdependent character of group life, and a well-defined sense of purpose help communities to meet individuals' needs and empower collective behavior.

At Messiah, for example, the use of small groups suited the charismatic emphasis on prayer. In charismatic fellowships members place considerable stress on praying frequently with others who share their burdens and joys. Each member is given the opportunity to share concerns so the other members can pray with the individual. Such personal attention would be impossible in a large group. Either the prayers would have to be abbreviated or the group would spend an interminable time giving everyone opportunity to speak. The smaller group structure therefore meets a practical need of the fellowship. Likewise the formation of communal life is a pragmatic as well as religious endeavor.[8]

The efficiency rationale for community applies to its mission as well as its internal life. John Perkins asserts the importance of community to Voice of Calvary goals when he writes,

> We had to be based in community because only that kind
> of intense interdependence—and actual sharing of our
> lives—could mold us into the kind of ministry team that
> could make a strong positive impact on our neighborhood.
> And we needed to be a Christian community because
> community would provide just the right kind of laboratory
> for working out the tough nitty-gritty of reconciliation.[9]

This "laboratory" function of community is a crucial reason for its existence. What religious communities seek to prove about Christian love and empowerment requires an intense and unequivocal commitment. The restricted agenda and limited variables of communal life provide the most favorable conditions for conducting a test of their religious insights.

Here we come to understand that communities do not view themselves as a superior expression of the church. This would be analogous to saying that in building a fire the kindling is superior to the logs. The small dry wood, however, serves a purpose to the logs and the achievement of fire. Likewise, the communities have a distinctive igniting role for the larger church. By force of their example they rekindle a passion for discipleship. Communities experience the call to a specific role—demonstrating the transforming power of faith when commitment to God is expressed through intense and intentional Christian fellowship. The routines that further career advancement and participation in the habits of an affluent society can so fragment individuals that the church receives only a small fraction of the remaining time and resources. After Christians have been drained by cultural demands they frequently lose the perspective and will to pursue the radical call of the gospel. The unqualified "yes" to God is compromised by competing interests. Eventually the great vision is reduced to what can be accomplished with the available time that is left.

The diminished vision breeds a people who come to know the gospel as appealing but unrealistic. Only a radical people can answer a radical call. The word *radical* comes from a Latin word which means "root." These Christian radicals want *to go back to the roots* of Christian faith. In the Acts church, they discover lifegiving principles that nourish contemporary Christian discipleship. They are also radicals in the sense that they choose *to pull up the roots* of society's customs that contradict Christian faith—roots that feed lifestyles of indifference to social wellbeing, and roots that feed policies of social injustice.

Clearly these communities are a radical departure from cultural trends, and they are a radical response to religious conviction. In choosing a simple lifestyle they manifest freedom from a materialism that drives and enslaves so many North Americans. By living among the poor they manifest reconciling love in a society that increasingly segregates the have-nots from the haves. By living communally they attest to the value of interdependence in a society that has venerated rugged individualism.

As discussed, the personal history of founders, the interpretation of biblical passages, and pragmatic advantages are integral to apprehending the call to community. This last consideration on the overwhelming influence of culture is crucial. One is not only called to community. One is also called out from a cultural identity that has values and loyalties which conflict with Christian vision. To be called from opulence to simplicity, from self-sufficiency to mutual dependency, from security to hostile environments of reconciliation and service is to become, by cultural standards, peculiar.

In the previous chapter John Winthrop was quoted as urging the new colonial settlers to be "a city upon a hill" so the world might be positively influenced by their example. He challenged them to be God's peculiar people. Similarly Clarence Jordan was convinced that a faithful community could serve a universal purpose.

> The ideas of God are constantly struggling for expression in the experiences of man. And before this new order can ever become a reality its got to take root in our own lives. Somewhere we've got to build a fellowship where men are transformed from the old things; where the old things pass away, and all things become new.[10]

Over 200 years apart, these two men articulate a common hope that their calling into a religious fellowship might fulfill the demands of discipleship and enable them to be a peculiar and redemptive presence in society.

In a Particular Place

Utopia, in Greek, literally means "nowhere" or "not a place." When Sir Thomas More wrote his book *Utopia* in 1516, he used the word to describe a perfect society that could not be identified with a known geographical area. Although the religious groups that are the focus of this study are often called utopian communities, the word utopia is inappropriate for characterizing them. The religious communities do not live under the pretense of being ideal or achieving perfection.

And most important, their identity is inextricably bound to being somewhere in particular. Location is an essential factor in understanding the formation and purpose of these groups. The history and social realities of the places they exist are integral to their calling.

Comparing the location decisions of these groups with those

of nineteenth-century communities further emphasizes the significance of place. In seeking an environment where they could experiment with religious and social principles, most of the nineteenth-century communes moved far from centers of social life. In the rural east and frontier west they found the isolation which was crucial to conducting their communal way of life. The religious communes could be devoted totally to achieving their vision without fear of interference from Christians who thought their beliefs heretical or public officials who thought their practices immoral and illegal.

The Christian communities of this investigation, however, are called to be in the midst of North America's social centers. Rather than virgin land, they seek territory trampled by the traffic of public life. Such places become the seedbed for their religious commitment.

The importance of place is evident in the brochure which first publicized the plans for Koinonia. The prospectus stated that the farm would probably locate in Georgia or Alabama "because of the poverty of the soil, and because of the need and neglect of the people, especially the Negroes." The community's location was not selected on the basis of environmental conditions that assured a protected and prosperous community. The location chosen had an environment in need of a community's care and resources.

Some biographical insights into Clarence Jordan suggest how such a concern for place developed. When Jordan was in high school, he was acutely aware of suffering in his vicinity caused by economic deprivation. He believed that through acquiring the skills of scientific farming he would be able to help poor farmers. To this end he continued his education by majoring in agriculture at the University of Georgia.

Although Jordan received a bachelor of science degree in agriculture, his assessment of social problems shifted from a strictly economic analysis to one that included the need for spiritual awakening. He therefore embarked on theological studies that culminated with a master of theology degree and a Ph.D. in New Testament Greek from Southern Baptist Theological Seminary (Louisville, Kentucky).

Jordan's passion for fighting injustice remained strong during this theological education. While doing his doctoral work, Jordan became involved in a social ministry in a black ghetto of Louisville. After recognizing that many of the impoverished he helped were forced off farms in Georgia and Alabama, he concluded, "The city was grinding them up. It drove me to get back to the areas that were vomiting these people up and see if we couldn't reverse the trend from the farms to the city."[11]

Jordan sought to tackle the fundamental causes of northern migration and urban squalor. The 440 acres he bought near Americus were to be the place from which various economic, educational, and religious programs would reach the people of that region.

John Perkins' founding of Voice of Calvary had a similar rationale for location. At age seventeen, Perkins left Mississippi because of brutal attacks on his family and the suffocating climate of racism. In California he began to achieve financial stability and felt secure in its more liberal social practices. At age twenty-seven, Perkins had a religious conversion that caused him to rededicate his life to Christ. The need to address the social problems of black people was also awakened. After talking with black youth, whose families had migrated from the South, and noting how bleak their future seemed, he concluded,

> Many of the problems in the ghetto, I was seeing, were really the unsolved problems of the South. This incident triggered a growing conviction that God wanted me to go back to Mississippi to identify with my people there, to help them break out of the cycle of despair—not by encouraging them to leave but by showing them new life right where they were.[12]

Perkins returned to live in Mississippi in 1960. Within two years he accepted the invitation to pastor a church in rural Mendenhall, Mississippi. This ministry eventually developed into sponsoring a daycare program, thrift store, adult education courses, economic cooperatives, and civil rights litigation. By 1973 Perkins felt he had accomplished his goal of leadership development in Mendenhall. He was convinced this indigenous leadership could only mature if he left, thus breaking the bonds of dependence on him.

But Perkins also had the dream of cultivating leadership throughout the United States. The constant flow of persons coming to Mendenhall to learn about its ministries and the enthusiastic response to his public speaking were evidence of a national hunger for leadership training.

Jackson, Mississippi, seemed the best place to establish this new thrust. It was a Southern city that would enable Perkins to maintain his commitment to the region and draw on contacts he had cultivated over the years. It had a college which might become an important resource to the study center he planned. And its impoverished black neighborhood could become the base and mission field of his ministry. The choice of Jackson came as a careful decision to match location with the demands of calling.

With Perkins and Jordan, however, the decision for a particular place was not merely biographically determined. Theirs was more than a response to sophisticated social analysis and a nostalgic feeling for one's roots. Both men declared that God had directed them to their places of service. They sensed a crisis that needed attention. Poverty and racism had infected the land and threatened to decimate life. To the spiritually sensitive this was not just a social crisis but also a religious crisis. Perkins' and Jordan's sense of calling to a particular place came as a mission to restore health to the land by a creative demonstration of faith.

The location of Patchwork Central was also influenced by the fact that Indiana was home for the founding members. The two couples (Ruth and John Doyle, Elaine and Phil Amerson) had intense discussions in college about being in ministry together.

Years later the opportunity developed. The Doyles were living in Evansville, where John served as a United Methodist Church pastor. Feeling their lives were at a turning point, they decided it was time to pursue the dream of community that had been so inspiring during their college years. They contacted Phil and Elaine Amerson, who were teaching in Atlanta, to ask the Amersons to join them in a new form of ministry.

Excited by the chance to be with their old friends in this adventure, the Amersons accepted the invitation. The Amersons likewise shared their plans with friends Nelia and Calvin Kimbrough, with whom they had organized a house church in Atlanta in 1976. The Kimbroughs were seeking to be involved in a neighborhood where their commitments to religious community and mission (in a multiracial and underprivileged context) could be pursued. Evansville appeared to be a promising location for living out their calling and using their talents. Consequently, Patchwork was born with a founding core of six members.

A significant factor in Phil Amerson's eagerness to join Patchwork was his desire to return to his home state. However, he was not motivated by the sense of crisis which characterized the returns home of Perkins and Jordan. Amerson's return fulfilled a longing to be with the people of southern Indiana because he closely identified with their attitudes and ways of living. He also felt this familiarity could be useful to developing a ministry involving local residents. Lastly, the size of Evansville made it an appealing location for the experiment in community.

Amerson was aware of communal efforts in large cities located in the East and West. But could a community model flourish within the distinctive social and political patterns of a small Midwest town? This was a question he wanted answered through the creation of Patchwork.

Church of the Messiah chose its location for different reasons. Messiah lacked the process of going home again. Messiah was a traditional church related to a specific neighborhood before adoption of the community model. Perhaps the primary question for Messiah was not "Where will we go?" but "Will we stay?"

Messiah was a dying church in a dying section of Detroit. Many churches in such circumstances are resigned to one of two options: either to end the church's existence and encourage members to join other congregations, or to move to another vicinity (usually suburbia) where there is increased potential for financial and membership growth. Messiah took neither option. The church was determined to serve in what appeared a moribund environment. This determination was a theological affirmation that God's will could be accomplished in this place. And a related affirmation was that God had called Messiah to a purpose in this place. These affirmations undergirded the conviction that a church was to serve the place in which it was located.

In securing Ron Spann, a black priest, the congregation and the Episcopal archdiocese were committed to exploring if Messiah could develop a viable ministry to its neighborhood. In addition, Spann's personal desire to serve in an African-American neighborhood, where he could contribute to its welfare and be nourished by African-American folk, was a significant commitment to place. Although Spann was not returning to home territory, Messiah's neighborhood was a context in which his racial identity took root.

Messiah's initial understanding of ministry to its neighborhood had none of the commitment to systemic change found in the other four communities. The church was surrounded by over twenty boarding houses for the elderly, the retarded, and the physically and emotionally handicapped. With the birth of the charismatic community at Messiah in 1971 came the outreach to the residents of these houses. Messiah's new mission of pastoral care to these residents declared that a Christian community was responsible for the welfare of its neighbors. However, it would be another five years before Messiah's vision of neighborhood ministry would include the need to challenge structures of injustice.

Although Sojourners began with a prophetic voice, its mission to a specific locale did not thrive until its pastoral care problems were resolved. The magazine preceded the formation of the community. The publication's wide circulation caused the growth of a national constituency before the community was established and local ministries developed. Sojourners' mission was more to issues than to a place.

When Sojourners' communal efforts in Chicago failed, the remnant of members searched for a new spirit of community and a new place to develop it. The Chicago neighborhood in which they were located was changing from low-income to middle-class people, so the members had little interest in remaining there. Most of the magazine's supporters were located in the

eastern section of the country. The idea of moving close to people who shared enthusiasm for their work eventually led to
Washington, D.C., as the community's new home.

The conversations with Graham Pulkingham had given the
community a new sense of how essential pastoral care was to the
quality of their fellowship. They resolved problems of intimacy
with one another and went to Washington determined to nurture their relationships. Their convictions about identifying with
the poor led them to choose a low-income neighborhood for
their residential life. They also became deeply involved in relationships with the people of this area and the social issues which
affected them. While identification with the poor had been part
of members' personal relationships in Chicago, it was not until
the move to Washington, D.C., that Sojourners created ministries specifically for poor neighbors.

This synopsis of communal beginnings makes clearer how
location for these religious communities is not incidental; rather,
it is a crucial factor in the communities' reason for being. The
emphasis on place can be traced to the assertion that a religious
fellowship is an expression of the body of Christ. The life and
ministry of Jesus are the example of what this body of Christ
should do. Jesus formed a fellowship of disciples who were to
proclaim and bear witness to the coming realm of God. Religious
communities therefore see their role as bringing people into relationships where they can experience the love of a dawning
new order. Jesus was clear about the revolutionary nature of his
calling when he read,

> The Spirit of the Lord is upon me, because he has anointed
> me to preach good news to the poor. He has sent me to
> proclaim release to the captives and recovering of sight to
> the blind, to set at liberty those who are oppressed, to pro-
> claim the acceptable year of the Lord. (Luke 4:18-19)

Religious communities understand their mission as addressing
the powers and principalities that have a death grip on the poor
and oppressed.

A seminal discussion of Jesus' relationship to the poor and

oppressed is in Howard Thurman's *Jesus and the Disinherited.* Thurman develops the thesis that God's message of hope was communicated to the disinherited through one (Jesus) who was also disinherited. Jesus' status as a poor and oppressed Jew enabled him to identify with the severity of those who suffered and stood "with their backs against the wall."[13] Jesus' message to the disinherited was to empower them to overcome the oppressive forces that tormented their lives. Amidst the wounded, oppressed, and despairing, one comes to comprehend more fully the meaning and power of Jesus' faith. The faith of Jesus can be best understood within the type of context in which it was first forged and expressed.

These selected communities have been convicted by such an understanding. All are located in areas where the residents are mainly poor and black. This intentional proximity to the poor and oppressed is the communities' way of identifying with them—and following the example of Jesus.

In the four urban communities, such a commitment has been a mixed blessing. Members experience warm and lasting relationships with their neighbors. After learning to take precautions against crime, and after establishing deep relationships with neighbors, some members become quite attached to their location and truly consider it home. However, the location has also been difficult for many members and has kept potential members from joining. Persons feel fear and anxiety in neighborhoods where they are a white minority and crime is common.

Such feelings are not unwarranted. In two of the communities members have been raped. Almost every home in the urban communities has been burglarized. Some members have been victims of armed robbery. White members have frequently been the targets of verbal abuse, usually about race, as they walk through their neighborhood. The perception that their neighborhood is hostile and unsafe adds tension and anxiety to communal life.

The communities take seriously the danger of their location and try to keep the danger from becoming an obsession. These negative factors, however, are the reality in which the poor and oppressed live. By accepting this reality as the reality of the community, the members' commitment to identify with the poor and oppressed takes on integrity. They may not like living in these neighborhoods, but they accept their location as a condition of membership and as a crucial place from which to understand how to be in mission.

The communities' commitment to place affirms the biblical paradigm of love being directed to specific contextual realities. The Scriptures disclose how God's interaction with God's people is sensitive to their particular experience in particular places. Love and place are bound together.

In *The Land,* Old Testament scholar Walter Brueggemann argues persuasively that any conception of God making covenant with people must also include a concern for their location. He says there is a "preoccupation of the Bible for placement." And that "land is a central, if not *the central theme* of biblical faith." The necessity of this perspective to the Judeo-Christian concept of covenant comes forth as Brueggemann concludes, "It will no longer do to talk about Yahweh and his people but we must speak about Yahweh and his people *and his land* . . . his promise for his people is always his land."[14]

This view of covenant functions in the communities' sense of call. The locations of their ministry and the welfare of the places they serve are essential to the fulfillment of their calling. The call to community is a call to be passionate about the welfare of a particular place.

To an Unknown Future

The call to community is an invitation to serve God through intimate fellowship and mission. Such an invitation, however, is not a blueprint which outlines the specifics of a community's work, nor is there the assurance of success. This explanation dispels the notion that the call is a clarion directive, with detailed designs of action which guarantee a definite future.

An anecdote from Patchwork's beginnings illustrates the point. The founders of Patchwork realized they were unprepared to determine the type of structure and work that should define their community. So they agreed to be deliberate about charting the community's course of development. They decided to defer making decisions that defined the community until they had completed four months of being in fellowship together. Still outsiders who heard about the founders coming together were intrigued by the idea of community and wanted to participate in this new venture. One evening the founding members were on the front porch drinking beer when one of these interested persons came by and asked if his church's youth group could come see their ministry. In their reclined and relaxed state the founders could only reply, "This is it, folks."

The effort to determine what the call to community means can provoke a major crisis for a fellowship. As discussed earlier, the intense philosophical and emotional investment of Sojourners' members in developing their Chicago community led to the group's dissolution. While the birth of a community is often a difficult time, as members try to clarify their purpose, concern over proper interpretation of a community's call continues as long as it exists.

This desire to be sure that a community is true to its calling can create conflicts that threaten its harmony and survival. Even with the threat, the task of clarifying purpose must be done. The extensive amount of time and energy given to these matters indicates how the initial sense of being called to community does not provide a blueprint for the future. Besides an ambiguity about what the fellowship should be and do, communities embark upon their ministry without a vision of how their future will unfold.

This is not to say that members are without plans and expectations. As stated, often the strong convictions about the direction of a community lead to division and, ultimately, to its demise. Still, the communities do not commence their life with a divine preview of the future that reassures their sense of calling.

The changing tides of life at Koinonia reveal how communal realities can deviate from initial conceptualizations of community. Martin England and Clarence Jordan envisioned a place of many persons with diverse skills who would come and contribute to Koinonia's fellowship and mission. They anticipated that this would not occur immediately, but they did not expect the erratic membership patterns that would impair Koinonia's development.

After two years of working with the Jordans at the farm, the Englands accepted a missionary assignment in Burma. This left the Jordans at the farm alone. The first permanent residents did not arrive at Koinonia until 1948, six years after the community's founding. Each year after 1948 saw a steady increase in membership. By 1950 there were fourteen adults and several children, and in 1953 the fellowship had nineteen adults and twenty-two children. Then, after years of violent attacks, a slow attrition in membership began. By 1968 the farm had only two couples again.

Besides membership, Koinonia struggled with far different matters than the educational and economic cooperative plans of Jordan and England. In 1956 Clarence Jordan agreed to sign application forms that would allow two black students to be considered for enrollment at the all-white Georgia State College of Business Administration. The students requested his support because their applications required the recommendation of two graduates of the Georgia University system. When the executive secretary of the Board of Regents declared Jordan's support invalid, since he was a graduate in Agriculture instead of Business, Jordan returned to Americus without signing the applications.

News spread throughout Americus, however, that Jordan was attempting to challenge the segregated practices of the region. Soon Koinonia experienced anonymous telephone threats; cancellation of insurance on equipment and property; an economic boycott whereby local merchants would no longer sell farm supplies to Koinonia nor market its products; the bombing of its properties; members being harassed, assaulted, jailed, and shot at; the intimidation of children in school; and legal action to terminate the community.

The original vision for Koinonia was cooperation with its neighbors in living out Christian principles of caring and sharing. This vision of harmonious relationships was shattered as Koinonia's efforts to express Christian caring led to placing the community under a state of siege.

The dramatic altering of an anticipated future is also evident with Church of the Messiah. The community began as a charismatic fellowship that stressed pastoral care for neighbors. Within five years, the concerns of the fellowship included the development of inner-city housing and a peace ministry in which members practiced civil disobedience against military armaments.

Many members who joined Messiah to praise God in a charismatic fellowship felt betrayed by the evolution into social and political activism. The neighborhood was also an insecure environment for members. Members who primarily envisioned themselves as being part of the church had to come to grips with being residents of a poor, predominantly black, crime-ridden neighborhood. The threatening nature of the area resulted in many members leaving Messiah.

In answering the call to community, members often do not realize how uncertain and volatile their future will be. This is, however, the biblical nature of call. When God enlists servants there is neither a bill of particulars about our involvements, nor is there the guarantee that our expectations will be fulfilled. The future is God's, and God does not make it conform to human desire. Jonah discovered this verity when Ninevah, to Jonah's lament, escaped God's wrath and destruction. Even Jesus, according to Clarence Jordan, did not know how his experiment with kingdom of God ideas would come out.

The response to God's call is "yes." The yes is the willingness to submit to God. It is not a conditional willingness, but one which accepts that we are called by Mystery into mystery. God will not be disclosed fully. And those who accept God's call have the privilege of affirming their faith—not in a God who can be manipulated to fulfill our expectations, but in the God whose answer to our most penetrating questions about God's nature is, "I will be what I will be" (Exod. 3:14).

The call to community is a call to the mystery of intimacy and mission. It is an intimacy with others that ruptures isolation so that love flows. It is an intimacy with God so that God's compassion is experienced, and so that life might be filled with joy and a peace that passes all understanding. And it is a call to mission

that seeks to reconcile the broken harmony of the social order—a mission that serves God through responsible stewardship of the earth.

This response to God's call may lead to persecution, disappointment, and the valley of the shadow of death. Or it may lead
to the joys of intimacy and celebrations of social transformation.
The history of these religious communities testifies to this fact.
We cannot count on a future full of jubilation, nor can we be certain of a future full of troubles. The only assurance about the future is that God's love will be steadfast. To the faithful in religious communities, this is sufficient.

For the Church Today

The renewal of the church is dependent on its ability to *listen*.
Considering how often we hear religious leaders imploring the
church to *speak* to the world, the necessity to listen may seem
odd. The church is asked to proclaim its gospel message with
bold assurance that it has the answer to the problems that keep
the world in turmoil. Although the church is to be a herald of
God's good news, its speech must be informed by what it has
heard. Before we speak, we must listen.

The primary question for a congregation is this: How has the
congregation *heard* the call of God? This question probes a congregation's awareness of its identity and purpose. Just because a
congregation calls itself a Christian church and may be affiliated
with a denomination, its awareness of its identity and purpose
cannot be presumed. The bane of many congregations is that
their identity and purpose have resulted from poor hearing.
They have not distinguished the call of God from the call of other gods. Consequently their congregational witness has been
conditioned by social and political interests that do not reflect
God's intent for the world.

H. Richard Niebuhr, in his classic book, *The Social Sources of
Denominationalism*, laments that the church has "compromised"
its ideals. This compromise has fueled the formation of many denominations. He concludes,

The division of the churches closely follows the division of men into the castes of national, racial, and economic groups. It draws the color line in the church of God; it fosters the misunderstandings, the self-exaltations, the hatreds of jingoistic nationalism by continuing in the body of Christ the spurious differences of provincial loyalties; it seats the rich and poor apart at the table of the Lord, where the fortunate may enjoy the bounty they have provided while the others feed upon the crusts their poverty affords.[15]

When the church makes these compromises, it betrays its calling to be God's obedient people. This betrayal results in the church losing that true sense of identity and purpose essential to renewal.

Our churches are filled with people whose lives are dominated by powerful forces of a modern technical society. These forces often cause persons to believe that some compromise of Christian values is necessary for survival in this highly competitive world. Their lives are fragmented by the need to serve many different loyalties. Materialism, self-indulgence, cut-throat business practices, and social climbing snare Christians as readily as anyone else in society. Sadly, Christians also often carry these values with them as they conduct the business of the church.

The challenge before the church is to shape an identity of discipleship which resists succumbing to values contrary to the Christian faith. In doing this, the church need not attempt to isolate its members from modernity and society, but it should help them be a prophetic witness to culture. Christian disciples are a public people. They celebrate being *in* God's world, yet they are a peculiar people who are not *of* it.

The selected religious communities in this book are able to isolate and critique those cultural values which are in conflict with the Christian faith. And they avoid being seduced into a cultural church. The factors that inform the intentional communities' sense of call are also instructive for local congregations. They suggest how a fellowship might hear clearly and respond faithfully to the call of God.

• *We are called by God to be a peculiar people.* As explained, personal history, Scripture, and pragmatism are sources that have been crucial to the formation of communities as alternative contexts of meaning. A local congregation can use these sources to amplify its calling.

We examined how the personal history of the communities' founders informed their passion to establish fellowships of radical discipleship. Within their life stories we find painful and inspiring experiences that shaped their decision to form communities of intimate caring and social witness. Their commitment was a response to their history. Such a response is a religious act, for personal history is sacred story. The founders' history was for them a living text of God's involvement with their lives.

Their conviction about their history is confirmed by one of the first lessons we are taught in Bible study—God is the God of history. Our task is to cultivate within a congregation the importance of remembering and interpreting history so the saving acts of God are not lost to the past. The church brings the past into its life through the reading of Scriptures, the reenactment of rituals, the professing of creeds. But in addition to the rich past of Christendom, every member and every local congregation has a sacred past that requires remembering and interpretation—a past capable of providing meaning and direction for a congregation's present witness.

The past can both impede and enliven a congregation's response to God's call. I have been surprised to find churches with only five or six members that have no intention to merge with other churches or to close. Why? For the remaining members this is the place of grandparents and parents. They feel an obligation to keep the fellowship going once a week. Those long dead have passed them the mantle to continue operating the church. In many of these churches, members no longer feel the vitality of fellowship and worship but continue to function as a church to control the church cemetery. This suggests how strong the influence of the past can be on a congregation. Maintaining a habitat for the dead can be more compelling than beginning a new future for the living. And whether it is the wisest decision or not, many congregations will declare a holy war against denominational authorities, pastors, and laity who try to terminate their local church.

This urge to make the church a museum of a previous time surfaces in small and large congregations in a variety of ways. When some congregations are faced with decisions about their future, the membership engages in a nostalgic recalling of the "glory days"—when the membership was growing, the Sunday school classes were numerous and full, the preaching was dynamic, the youth group was active, and the choir's singing inspired. Or congregations might be caught in the "we have never done it that way" syndrome. Consequently, suggestions about changing the liturgy or initiating new church programs fall on deaf ears.

The past is not meant to be a source of traditions and events that the church embalms. The past contains a history that is most revered when it is recalled and interpreted to energize the church to meet its new challenges. The God of history is not time bound. The vitality of God expresses itself in every age. Disciples therefore must be responsive to a God not only of the past, but also of the present and future.[16]

We must help our churches remember how God has been active in their past so that they recognize the present and future call of God. Whether in Sunday school classes, worship, study groups, or administrative boards and conferences, the local church can engage in the exercise of remembering. Through such an exercise of remembering, it can seek to *hear* God's call to be a peculiar people.

On a personal level some questions of remembering might include these: Have the expectations for Christian discipleship ever seemed clear to you? When were you most faithful to the sense of divine call? When were you not true to the call of God? Have you sometimes felt that the expectations for discipleship were too demanding? How did you resolve this? Have you ever felt you missed opportunities of discipleship? What caused you to miss them? Have you been disappointed that God did not act as you expected? What was/is your reaction to a time or times of disappointment? When has God's activity surprised you?

Here are questions for the congregation: Why was this congregation established? How has our present identity been shaped by the commitment of the forebears of this congregation? What is God's purpose for this church? Do we have a past that suggests we know how to be a peculiar people? When have we been most proud of the way we cared for one another in this church? What are the most inspiring and embarrassing times of our history? Why do they inspire or embarrass us? How might we try to redeem the unfaithful times of our past?

Discussing such questions is an effort to get members talking about their identity as a called people, and to attune each member to God's persistence. Member identity is not just a matter of being on a congregation's membership roles but is grounded in the reality of God's claim. Members' purposes are not determined just by what they feel comfortable doing but are grounded in God's love for the world.

It is easy for a church, however, to remember only its own history as the basis for understanding its identity and purpose. When this occurs, a church reduces religious truth to its *experience* of truth. The faith of the ages is transformed to comply with the memory of a congregation's history. A church then becomes an orphan of the past.

Relying on the Scriptures connects a church with its roots. The Scriptures are necessary for more completely understanding the call of God. They reveal God to us in a history before our history. They tell the story of the beginnings of our religious heritage. They disclose how God has always been in search of a servant people. They reveal the insights for discipleship we might receive by knowing the responses of our religious ancestors to God's search. The renewal of a congregation is dependent on its ability to *hear* God's call in the Scriptures.

In *Jesus and Community*, New Testament scholar Gerhard Lohfink writes about the New Testament churches' efforts to live the message of Jesus. Their commitment led them to develop fellowships where members nurtured one another and rejected social bigotry. Lohfink describes these churches as having a climate of caring, making them often exemplary of God's will for human relationships. They were contexts where "wonders" occurred because members had accepted the gospel as the authority over their fellowship. Lohfink makes an instructive connection for the church today—when the church gives itself to the authority of the gospel, it experiences extraordinary power to heal the brokenness in persons, its fellowship, and society.[17]

A congregation might consider focusing its Bible study on the theme of hearing the call of God—asking itself if the call heard by the New Testament churches is also the call for the church today. Does God still call the church to create a fellowship where the resources of each member are given for the welfare of all? Does God still call the church to be an alternative to a social order of oppression and injustice? How does the witness of the New Testament churches inform the church's witness today? How is their story our story?

These questions lead a congregation to listen to the Scriptures for a word about their peculiar identity and purpose. And to hear within the Scriptures, stories of Christians accepting the call to radical discipleship. Another question which arises from such listening is this: Does God continue to call us to such radical obedience? This question offers the possibility that Christians today might be relieved from the difficult demands of caring and social transformation that depict the call of New Testament churches. The question betrays the reluctance we often have to be called to radical acts of discipleship.

A sincere encounter with the Scriptures makes us accountable to a history and authority which transcend our willingness to do only what is enjoyable. Our obedience to God may be characterized more by sacrifice than by benefiting from an affluent society. Listening to the Scriptures will not only make us dissatisfied with what we are but will inspire us to become what God calls us to be.

The call to be a peculiar people does not mean that institutional churches are to become religious communities like Sojourners or Koinonia. But the call does require the institutional church to respond with all of itself. *The particular organization of the membership is not as important as its commitment.* In fact, if a congregation is reorganized such that it no longer even recognizes itself, the identity confusion will not help it achieve its purpose.

Radical discipleship is relevant discipleship. We will only be successful in achieving our purpose as God's church when we tailor our church structures with a sensitivity to the character of our religious fellowship and the demands of the places in which we serve.

• *We are called by God to a particular place.* The church is called to stewardship of God's sacred creation. For the institutional church, the environment served is especially determined by the church's location. Property defines a church as a neighborhood institution. Property is a visible sign of placement that suggests an identification with its surroundings.

After asking pastors to tell me about their ministry to their churches' community, I have been surprised to hear many say: "My *members* don't live in the area surrounding the church. Therefore my church's community is the various places where our members live." This answer fails to realize how the location of the church automatically defines its community.

We would think it irresponsible of a bank to make decisions about loans based on where its employees live. Banks are judged conscientious community institutions according to the extent of their investment in businesses and homes near the bank. Even when a bank claims that most of its customers do not come from its immediate area, there will be cries for the bank to be committed to the area in which the institution is located. Why? Because the *institutional* identity of the bank is related to its location. The place of institutional residence anchors its identity. And if a bank (through its investment practices) denies its neighborhood identity, the people in its immediate area will protest and pressure it to be a good neighbor.

Likewise a church's identity is established by its location. The church's identity is rooted in the land it occupies, and the church's mission is guided by the welfare of the territory that surrounds it. The question is not whether a church's community is its immediate neighborhood; this is a given. The only question is whether a church is a caring or negligent neighbor to its surrounding community. Using the bank analogy, the "investment" practices of local churches (through programming, time given, and financial decisions) affirm or negate their identity as caring neighbors.

The alienation of churches from their neighborhoods has caused many neighborhood residents to question these churches' commitment. Frequently churches seem interested in their neighborhoods only when they need members or support for a fundraising effort. Residents suspect that the neighborhood is perceived by the church as a source for its survival and that, as far as the church is concerned, the neighborhood has no value in itself.

A congregation might explore how its identity is tied to its environment by discovering why its church was established in its present location. Perhaps the placement of the church resulted from denominational planning to serve an increasing population where the denomination did not have an institutional presence. Or perhaps the church was established because in that sparsely populated and rural area a few families sacrificed to build a house of worship. The history of each congregation is distinctive. But within each history is usually a story of the church being organized because of a vision for ministry and mission to a particular place.

A congregation might ask itself if the original call to serve its vicinity is still operative. If not, what is the new call to its vicinity? If a congregation is considering moving to a new location, does this move result from a sense of God's call to a place? Or is the move due to fears and prejudices about present neighbors? A church's placement influences its witness. A congregation's decision to stay in or move from a location reflects on its identity as a faithful fellowship. Consequently, an acute awareness of the importance of place to a church's purpose is essential.

Without the conviction of being called to a particular place, a church may be seduced into relocating itself because a new neighborhood has an affluent and "acceptable" racial or ethnic population. Again this decision would be based upon what the neighborhood could do for the church. However, being fully responsive to God's call means that a congregation, like the religious communities of this study, should be open to moving from an affluent to a poor area—or from a neighborhood where most of the residents are "just like us" to one that places the congregation in relationship with residents whose race and culture are different than the congregation's.

Another seduction is for churches located in affluent and homogeneous residential areas to assume that their only community outreach must be to some destitute section of their region. These churches assume that the affluence of their area has immunized their residents against the need for outreach ministries. The churches keep a Pollyanna demeanor while spouse abuse, substance addiction, teenage suicide, and a plethora of other problems haunt the people of the community. Churches are called to serve the places where they are located. And while mission to a more destitute community is necessary and praiseworthy, it does not justify abandoning the welfare of one's own place.

The call to a particular place requires the church to listen to and be in caring relationship with the people of that place. Primary to the church's identity is its role as neighbor. Neighbors are not first known by investigation but by conversations. Our conversations are not marked by requesting data for problem solving, but by inviting others to experience the terrain of our heart. Problem solving may become the natural consequence of understanding and caring for one's neighbor, but it does not replace the forging of caring relationships.

The church is renewed through its involvements as neighbor. It experiences the power of renewal released when identity and purpose are fulfilled. That renewal is the result of being what God has called the church to be as God's peculiar people. Renewal also occurs because God is already in the community waiting to heal and empower the church. Long before any church has ventured into its locale to be neighborly, God has been actively caring for God's creation. God resides in the community that many churches fear. And so in outreach the church not only gives but receives.

In its *listening* to neighbors, the church will *hear* how God has sustained the destitute through the most desolate of times; how God has sustained individuals who have been besieged by one tragedy after the other; and how God is a source of hope to persons trapped in despairing conditions. The church is called to particular places, not only to be a force of renewal, but also to experience the renewing presence and power of God.

• *We are called by God to an unknown future.* The church has always had to answer its members' strong craving to know the future. This must have led Jesus to say, "Therefore do not be anxious about tomorrow, for tomorrow will be anxious for itself" (Matt. 6:34). This craving is more than normal anticipation of expected occurrences or preparation for the next generation; it is the effort to eliminate any uncertainty about the future's impact upon our lives. The uncertainty itself becomes the monster that is feared and attacked. Predictability is sought, whether through signs or the assertion of spiritual laws, as the bulwark against the future.

The explosive growth of many fundamentalist churches and the popularity of television evangelists is in part attributed to their theology of certainty. The believer is assured that life has joyous or despairing outcomes based on the believers' strict adherence to specified religious disciplines, professing of dogma, or flooding one's mind with positive attitudes. These religionists offer the promise of a religious formula that eradicates the need to fear uncertainty about matters of earth or heaven.

The craving for certainty is not just a trait of fundamentalist Christians or television audiences. All our churches have members who want assurances about their security and the church's security. This desire must be addressed by the institutional church with disciplines and a theology of faith that enable members to accept uncertainty as a given. In accepting uncertainty, they discover that their discipleship does not shrink before the challenges that call them to an unknown future.

The unknown future will not be entered faithfully if Christians are laden with the requirement to succeed with their ministry efforts. If we value only the accomplishment of successful results, then church members will be reticent to tackle concerns where success is not assured.

This problem is illustrated in an anecdote a pastor told me about his difficulties in recruiting members for various church committees. He was perplexed that members understood the importance of these committees but were still unwilling to invest time in them. At his church's annual retreat, the pastor told members how he had failed to achieve many goals he had set for himself the previous year. Despite these failures, he experienced the love of God and congregation in new and affirming ways.

At the conclusion of his confession, the pastor felt the members give a corporate sigh of relief, as if a heavy burden had been lifted from their hearts. Afterward members volunteered as never before for leadership positions in the church. When faithful effort replaced successful result as the test of discipleship, the members were liberated to serve.

Churches will also resist bold initiatives for the future because the churches' leadership is convinced that members do not want major demands made upon their time and resources. Therefore churches devise ministries that are the least controversial and consuming. But Rhodes Thompson, a Disciples of Christ minister, convincingly argues that the church underestimates the "latent heroism of the laity." Based on years of pastoral experience, he concludes that church members are hungry for a challenge worthy of their faith commitment. He has seen laity enthusiastic about ministries that might easily be dismissed as too demanding for a congregation.

God's peculiar people literally come to themselves in the intense labors of discipleship. Whether it occurs within a church committee or the whole congregation, the emergence of this heroism inspires a church. Formidable issues need not be barriers to ministry. The radical discipleship of laity is a source of renewal for the church.

Still, it must be remembered that faithful and heroic endeavors do not dispel uncertainty about the future. Our endeavors may lead us to a future of church celebration and community praise. They can also create congregational discord and the wrath of the community.

Ministry to the homeless and the emotionally disturbed are two concerns that have led churches to futures of conflict and celebration. I have heard the testimony of congregations that have claimed a greater awareness of Christian identity and purpose because of their work with the homeless or mentally ill.

They appreciate the support and accolades of the larger community for their commitment. Across town, another congregation experiences bitter internal division about involvement with such concerns. If they decide to establish a shelter for the homeless or a neighborhood residence for the mentally ill, they are confronted with angry neighbors who do not want the church to establish programs which bring "those kind of people" into the neighborhood. Caring does not provide an insurance policy for a future of harmony and appreciation. Our discipleship might intensify turmoil in our future.

God is our only certainty of the future. Pleasing God is the ultimate concern of our discipleship. Fears of failure, radical initiatives, harmony within our religious fellowship, and community approval are factors that require our sensitivity and wisdom. But they are not the reason we are called into God's future. We are called into the future to live out God's will for the future.

Rather than anticipating a future which obeys our demands for certainty, we can only be certain of finding God in a future that demands obedience. The call to be the church is the call to obedience. All of our preaching and teaching must help a congregation to accept and be responsive to this. Perhaps the question to ask ourselves is, Do we only want God to provide a future that we define? Is a future that submits to our terms the only future we choose to enter?

We try to domesticate God by making God serve our desires. But this is the folly of idolatry. God will be God regardless of our fears or courage about the future. The only real question does not revolve around squeezing more guarantees about the future from God but rather, will we be obedient to God? This is not a question to be negotiated, but to be answered "Yes" or "No."

CHAPTER 3

Living in Covenant

In Fellowship with Companions

Members of religious communities not only feel called to a particular place (i.e., neighborhood or county) for purposes of mission. They also sense that God calls them to participate in a religious fellowship where their peculiar identity as radical Christian disciples will flourish.

Their search for such a fellowship is propelled by four key convictions. First, they believe God has called them to a religious vocation. All other decisions about career, income, and (for some members) even family are secondary to maturing as a Christian whose whole life is given to serving God.

Second, membership in the institutional church is insufficient for preparing and exercising radical discipleship. A more intentional and intense commitment is necessary for full response to God's call.

Third, intentional religious community life is the crucible for their discipleship. Living in covenantal relationship with others who feel a similar call can empower their vocation. The call to a religious vocation is personal; God has invited each individual to labor in behalf of God's justice and love. The fulfillment of a religious vocation, however, is corporate. The complexity and difficulty of God's work requires a fellowship of discernment and cooperation.

Fourth, the development and empowerment of a corporate identity requires members to submit their lives to the order and disciplines of a religious community. Living in covenant requires structures which call for personal choices to be sacrificed for the sake of communal purpose.

Push and pull factors influence members' decision that a particular religious community is the context for practicing their vocation. Dissatisfaction with the institutional church is a major push to religious communalism. Before joining their present religious community, virtually all members were active in local congregations. At Koinonia Partners and Patchwork Central, most members continue to participate in the life of a local congregation other than that of the religious community. Whether they have a past or present involvement in the institutional church, these members conclude that the institutional church is not sufficiently oriented to enact fully the religious values of their vocation.

Reasons for dissatisfaction are many and varied. The most frequently listed complaints against the institutional church include lack of challenge for the demands of Christian faith, refusal to be involved in controversial social issues, worship that is too formal and impersonal, time and budgetary commitments devoted primarily to institutional maintenance, absence of activities leading to spiritual growth, and inability to foster intimate and caring relationships.

The institutional church, however, is more than the source of members' dissatisfaction. The church is also the *alma mater* of religious vision and ideals for Christian discipleship. Many members received their understanding of the Christian faith's radical message from institutional churches. Pulpits and Sunday school classes portrayed inspiring images of Christians deeply involved with one another's lives and boldly engaged in the social crises of God's world. The spiritual turmoil caused by churches whose witness retreated from enacting this radical message eventually led these members to seek another expression of God's church: intentional religious community.

Experience with a previous religious community is the other major push factor. In these five communities approximately one-third of members have belonged to other religious communities. Those who had a positive relationship with their former community sought the present religious fellowship as a context for continuing Christian growth. Usually they left their former community because their work required them to relocate or the community disbanded.

Those with a negative experience in their former community cite problems with authoritarian leadership, feelings of not being appreciated, the community's inability to respond to changing family needs, and the above complaints about the institutional church.

Whether the relationship with a previous community was positive or negative, a significant number of members continued to seek an intentional community because of prior experience. Their history in community pushed them to seek another communal fellowship.[1]

Intentional religious community as the most promising place to experience being totally committed to God is the major pull factor. Stories about the five communities this book explores are told in magazines, newspapers, and books. Sojourners' own magazine periodically describes life in its religious fellowship. All the communities have newsletters that communicate the successes and trials of community life. And community leaders are frequent guest speakers at church conferences. Audiences are inspired by their testimonies of how faith thrives through intentional community. Community members also indicate that they wanted to join their communities because of the testimonies of friends who belonged to the community.

The pull of intentional community results from the fundamental awareness that Christian faith is living not only in covenantal relationship with God but with companions of the faith pilgrimage. The call to community is experienced as the call to intimacy. Persons feel a deep urge to be bound to others in a nurturing and serving fellowship. They yearn for a Christian fellowship where a common commitment to spiritual growth, interpersonal nurture, and mission to peace and justice concerns forges their covenantal identity.

All the communities have covenantal statements that assert

theological beliefs, responsibilities of membership, and the principles for community organization. They expend much time and energy developing and periodically revising these statements. While these written covenants define communal identity and guide decision making, the truest understanding of living in covenant does not come from the stated affirmations. It is, rather, discovered in members' sense that their fellowship is characterized by commitment, trust, respect, and care. The opening sentences of the "Koinonia's Resident Partners' Covenant" represent the sentiments of the other four communities.

> We, the community of Resident Partners at Koinonia, seek
> by this covenant to record for ourselves and for others
> some of the basic affirmations that we hold in common.
> We do this recognizing that the richest and strongest
> bonds that unite us are personal and spiritual, not proposi-
> tional.

A community discovers that its efforts to live in covenant are more successful when it achieves an affirming environment rather than behavior dominated by affirmations.

Covenantal relationship, however, is not solely determined by *feelings* of intimacy and mission. Communities structure basic patterns of interaction that define their understanding of covenant. Living arrangements of members are one structured definer of covenantal relationship. Structuring of living arrangements reveals how home and family are related to covenantal commitments of intimacy and mission.

Koinonia, Sojourners, and Messiah established the extended household for their communities. Under this arrangement many people from different families lived in one housing unit. During 1979, for example, Sojourners averaged about ten adults and two children for each housing unit. At its membership peak, Messiah averaged sixteen persons per household; some households had as many as twenty-five people.

These were large homes with three to six bedrooms. Families usually had their own sleeping quarters but shared use of all other living space. Meals were scheduled so that most of the household could eat together. And responsibilities for preparing the meals and other household duties were rotated among household residents.

Extended households were organized for three primary reasons. First, the extended households were perceived to be the most appropriate context for members to know and care for one another. The households were not just places to eat, relax, and sleep. They were also the crucible for forging relationships and testing members' ability to function as a family. Here one's behavior was scrutinized under the pressure of living closely with others. The intense living situation enabled residents to become familiar with each other's strengths and weaknesses. Daily advice regarding personal and spiritual growth could be given. Such living also fostered a context where members could give in-depth care for each other on a regular basis. The extended households were the locus for nurturing intimacy.

Second, the extended households were formed for a pragmatic reason. Buying the large structures was the most affordable way to house the communities' members. Purchasing and renovating these buildings was less expensive than renting or buying space for each family. And it was more economical to buy major appliances for several families in one house than for each family in several locations.

Third, the extended households aided the communities' economic order and goals. The common treasury provided a modest living allowance for each member. Within an extended household one could stretch this amount, since many people would be using the same utilities or buying certain foods in quantity. A successful household required extensive scheduling, planning, compromising, and coordination. One learned how to share limited space and appliances to achieve simple living through interdependence.

Use of extended households in these communities has ended. Presently members live in houses or apartments as single families or individuals. A family might share space with one or two single persons. Or an apartment might house two single members. But these communities no longer have the large extended households that characterized their beginnings.

Several factors contributed to termination of extended households. Primary was the realization that home was becoming a place where one could not relax. Members felt households were a context of constant pressure where they had to relate to needs of other household members even if they longed to withdraw for awhile. Other members were involved in the disciplining of children even if that was not desired by the parent. One had to adjust emotionally to a dynamic of unfamiliar persons continually joining the household and friends continually leaving it. And the lack of privacy with spouse was not helpful for resolving marital problems.

At Messiah, for example, the members sought to care for one another by organizing their extended households into therapy settings. They thought members would benefit from ongoing household counseling. In time this proved unbearable. One household gathered at 6:00 a.m. to discuss spiritual concerns and interpersonal conflict. The intense and critical sessions left some feeling depressed. They soon realized that predawn mutual criticism was not the most inspiring way to start a day.

Messiah concluded that when households were used for therapy, members felt constantly under a microscope. Every word and act was subject to analysis. Messiah therefore decided that while households could be places of care, this did not have to include rigorous counseling. Like Sojourners and Koinonia, they became aware of the need for home to be a place of privacy, rest, and play.

Also at Messiah scheduling, counseling, and meetings of extended households were often the responsibility of individuals who directed these activities in an authoritarian manner. The complexity of household life seemed to demand decision makers who could address needs and problems decisively so a prolonged conflict would not exist. Household leaders would therefore establish procedures and areas of responsibility to quickly address the numerous concerns that surfaced.

When leaders assumed household members should submit to their decisions without question, extended household living became oppressive for some residents. Messiah reduced the size of its households since such a complex living arrangement often resulted in dictatorial household leadership and interpersonal tension. However, this revision of structure was not enough to compensate for the anger and disappointment persons felt toward the community. Because of their negative experiences with extended household living, some members left the community.

These problems of group pressure and household leadership were demoralizing, but the demise of extended households was ultimately the result of communities realizing that this living arrangement inhibited intimacy instead of promoting it. Members at Sojourners complained that while the activities and time requirements of extended households helped them to know residents of their house, they had less time to become intimate with community members in other households. Consequently, the household arrangement was bonding intimate relationships on a residential basis rather than fulfilling the goal of intimacy throughout the community.

The communities also discovered that the intensity of relationships in extended households sometimes led to alienation among members. Persons who ordinarily would have related well were in conflict because of efforts to live together.

This is not to say that extended households failed to create in-depth relationships. Extended households helped bond relationships, effect an environment of intense care, and forge a communal identity. But while extended households may have been the right choice for a community's beginning, the time came when problems outweighed the advantages. Extended households lost their mystique as an essential structure for communal intimacy and mission.

Voice of Calvary and Patchwork never saw extended households as a necessary structure of community. Two or three single people might live together at VOC, but this was more a matter of limited housing and economic advantage than fostering intimacy. Since 1986 the Antioch Community has been an extended family household that emanated from the Voice of Calvary Fellowship. In 1993 the six adults and two children were a stable group that used a common treasury economic arrangement. However, this household was the choice of the participating members rather than a requirement of the religious fellowship.

The Patchwork founders began their community fully aware of the pitfalls of extended households. They were especially concerned that such a living arrangement would interfere with the nurture of their nuclear families.

All five communities have encouraged intimacy by requiring members to live geographically near one another. They have also required members to reside in the communities' area of mission. This residency requirement has been essential to the communities' effort to live in covenant with the people to whom they minister, especially the poor and oppressed.

However, when Patchwork (1984) and Messiah (1987) restructured, these residency requirements were dropped. The two communities continued to emphasize physical proximity to their area of mission as the *preferred* residential location of members.

The economic structure of communities is a significant indicator of how work, resources, and stewardship are involved in the understanding of covenantal relationship. The financial arrangements of communities are devised to meet expenses, and they signify the nature of members' commitment to community. The economic order of communities requires members to adopt modest spending patterns and work cooperatively with others in determining purchases and scheduling the use of common property. They must modify their lifestyle and assess whether resources are invested in ministries that reflect the social imperatives of their calling.

Early in their histories, Koinonia, Sojourners, and Messiah employed the common treasury as their financial system. Under this system, the income and expenses of each individual belonged to the fellowship. The communities referred to the book of Acts, which describes how the Christians of Jerusalem organized their life together, as their model for Christian community.

> Now the company of those who believed were of one
> heart and soul, and no one said that any of the things
> which he possessed was his own, but they had everything
> in common. . . . There was not a needy person among
> them, for as many as were possessors of lands or houses

sold them, and brought the proceeds of what was sold and laid it at the apostles' feet; and distribution was made to each as any had need. (Acts 4:32, 34-35)

Community income was derived from several sources: the financial assets of newcomers, members' wages, and community businesses and ministries. At Sojourners and Messiah, a major contribution to the treasury came from members who worked outside of communal ministries. Their employment usually paid higher wages (in such fields as social work, teaching, and medicine) than the stipends given to members who worked in communal programs. Minor financial crises arose when these members no longer provided this income from well-paying jobs because of job dissatisfaction, desire to quit work and pursue more education, wanting to be involved in the community's ministries, or severing their relationship with the community.

Sojourners, Messiah, and Koinonia insisted that donations for and profits from ministries were *not* to be used to meet the financial needs of communal living. Money received from Koinonia's low-income housing program went back into the housing budget. Sojourners refused to use profits from its successful magazine to alleviate the financial pressures of the fellowship's living expenses. And Messiah separated its Common Life finances from those of the church and its ministries. In fact, occasionally the church was able to meet its budget only because of economic support *from* the Common Life group.

This separation of finances had three effects. First, it enabled communities to keep the focus of their work on service. Any suggestion that ministries were developed to sustain the financial needs of the fellowship would undermine a community's sense of call. It would imply that a community's work was motivated more by profit than prophetic caring. The communities labored so that others' needs were met, not to enhance the economic stability of their own fellowship.

Second, the communities stressed the importance of members' dependence on one another for their livelihood. The interdependent nature of a fellowship would be threatened if a substantial amount of income was received from sources other than what members brought from their labor. Significant interaction had to occur for a community to live off its members' income. History records the termination of many communities that were economic successes but failed to sustain a cooperative environment.

Third, a community's work ethic could be undermined by income not tied to members' labor. The need to work helped a community identify with the plight of humanity. It kept a fellowship's consciousness lodged in the reality of needing to develop skills, services, products, and relationships that enabled members to earn income. Clarence Jordan refused to accept a potential member's assets of about $90,000. He said that if Koinonia received her money "we'd quit growing peanuts and start discussing theology."[2]

Fourth, the commitment to a simple lifestyle would be threatened by substantial income from outside sources. Living with limited resources was not only an act of necessity but a witness of Christian stewardship. Even if a community did not spend the money, just having it available would contradict simple living. When a member of Sojourners was the beneficiary of a huge life insurance policy, the community devised ways for that money to go to nonprofit organizations that worked for peace and justice.

This commitment to restricting the sources of income and to a simple lifestyle meant that members lived within very modest budgets. The living allowances were below figures associated with families in poverty. In 1983 at Sojourners, the monthly allowance averaged $350 a person. In 1986 at Koinonia, the monthly allowance averaged $250. These small allowances were supplemented by the common treasury, which covered expenses for housing, utilities, transportation, medical needs, and appliances. In addition, communal gardens and bulk food purchases helped stretch the allowances.

Even with the community taking responsibility for major costs, living within such modest budgets was still difficult. Those with children found that clothing needs often escalated beyond the budget. This was especially true if children wanted new garments as opposed to used ones. Children also wanted the games, toys, records, and entertainment opportunities of peers who did not live in a religious community.

One adult member who left Sojourners indicated that financial restrictions prevented her from expressing affection to people through gifts. Gifts had always been a major way for her to show people that she cared about them, and this was no longer possible under the tight Sojourners budget. She felt humiliated the day she needed to borrow money to send her father a birthday card. Communities lost members like her who could not or chose not to adjust to the requirements of a common treasury.

Over the years these communities made changes in their approach to the common treasury. At one point all of Koinonia's members would discuss a person's needs and decide how to expend money. Now, a resident partner presents his or her projected needs to an economic coordinator who works with the partner to establish a reasonable and equitable allowance.

After six years of common treasury, Sojourners shifted more expenditures from the community account to each person's living allowance. Members felt that covering too many financial obligations from a common treasury bred childlike dependency. In 1989 Sojourners terminated its common treasury. Members now tithe, from salaries earned in community ministries or employment elsewhere, into a treasury used for emergency assistance and the maintenance of household property still communally owned. When Messiah ended its Common Life structure in 1987, the common treasury also ended.

The discipline necessary to make a common treasury work is perceived to indicate a more intense communal commitment. Communities still extol the value of this economic arrangement for being a covenant fellowship. However, like the break from extended households, some aspects of common treasuries were more harmful than helpful in enabling intimacy and mission.

One member who left Messiah's Common Life arrangement said that many of the efforts toward economic cooperation did little to bring people closer together. Important matters of intimacy were not addressed by increasing members' financial interdependence. In time, communities came to realize that everyone need not be part of economic decision making for the community to share financial burdens.

Patchwork Central and Voice of Calvary never used the common treasury as an economic structure of community. Patchwork members began by contributing 3 percent of their income from employment to their corporate ministry. This was revised to an amount each member determines to reflect his or her commitment. Members of the Voice of Calvary Fellowship have always been expected to tithe (understood to be at least 10 percent of income). Although persons were not forced to tithe, the standard has been stated so strongly members experience it as a requirement of membership.

At Patchwork and VOCF, the time and energy given to developing a strong financial base for ministry influenced intimacy more than a structure that governed personal finances. The economic emphasis of these two communities has been on funding that enables them to implement their programs. Economics have been structured for outreach, not for an interdependence that fosters intimacy.

The three communities with common treasuries were no more successful at intimacy and mission than those with a different economic structure. Often the complexity of common treasury arrangements siphoned emotional energy and time away from mission and interpersonal relationships. Anxiety about this economic arrangement caused many individuals not to join these communities. Dissatisfaction with the common treasury resulted in members leaving community, or if they stayed, being frustrated with financial decisions.

At the same time, the use of such an economic system often gave members a sense of being bound to one another. They found strength for simple living through participation in such an economic agreement. Koinonia bears witness to this conviction with its continuing use of the common treasury.

Where a common treasury was not used, a community was saved from being embroiled in exhausting economic procedures. However, more weight fell on other structures of commitment (such as social activism and nurture groups) to instill the cooperation and sacrifice essential to living in covenantal fellowship.[3]

Interdependence is an important characteristic of covenant. Communal gardens, the economics of a common treasury, and shared use of communal properties (homes, automobiles, lawn mowers, freezers, washers, dryers) make negotiation, coordination, and cooperation essential qualities of communal life. Interdependence is instrumental to covenant but is not the covenant itself. Ultimately, the sense of living in covenant is determined by the belief that one is in fellowship with companions (who value intimate caring relationships) in the adventure of becoming radical Christian disciples.

To Be Known and Loved

Individuals seek to be in a fellowship where they are called by name and where they receive the care of its members. Living in covenant is more than cooperation in work, housing, and economics. Members expect to feel embraced by each other as they pursue communal goals. In addition to the routines of work and meetings, they want a time with others when personal and interpersonal concerns (regarding emotional and spiritual matters) are the sole focus of their gathering.

Many join religious communities with high expectations that such times will be a regular occurrence. Others may not have joined a community for personal care, but the demands of communal life make attending to the personal dimension a pressing need. In both cases, the plea is for a community to be as intentional about members' inner life as it is toward communal organization and mission matters.

Throughout its history, Koinonia's members have accused the community of being inattentive to personal growth and group intimacy. The community responded by recommitting itself to group processes that encouraged members to communicate their feelings with one another. This response, however, often failed to satisfy the appeal for help in cultivating personal and interpersonal life in the community. Thus members left the community in search of a place which could better meet their needs.

Some members believe that the inadequate attempts to create structures of personal support and group cohesion reflect a lukewarm commitment to intimacy. While this may be partly true, Koinonia's difficulties are also testimony to the fact that caring for the emotional needs of persons is complicated. Good intentions do not necessarily equip a group to navigate the perplexing terrain of the inner self.

The Voice of Calvary Ministries is so oriented to providing economic and social services that matters of intimacy are not a structured part of the organization. Its church, the VOC Fellowship, has created a small group structure to provide members a more intimate context to address concerns. However, within these small groups members have been primarily involved in Bible study, prayer, and faith development. Personal matters related to members' spirituality are dealt with, but emotional and relational concerns are not usually addressed. A member can make an appointment for counseling with the Fellowship's pastors. Otherwise, counseling is not shared by the membership.

Patchwork has also not been deeply invested in structuring ongoing intensive opportunities to address personal and interpersonal concerns. The lack of commitment to such matters precipitated a crisis; half of the members left. One of Patchwork's founders was involved in counseling even before the community's inception. However, because he was an active participant in Patchwork's struggles, the community did not consider him a neutral resource to mediate conflict and to develop ways members could focus on pastoral care to one another.

Patchwork now has a pastoral team (five to seven members) that focuses on personal and interpersonal issues that may erupt into communal conflict. The desire for ongoing structured experiences of emotional counseling, spiritual guidance, or relationship enhancement has not been an overwhelming mandate from members, even though the interpersonal issues are often so intense as to threaten the well-being and existence of the community.

Three Patchwork members are United Methodist ministers; recognizing the important ministry of Patchwork, their denomination has endorsed their involvement in Patchwork by appointing them to the community. Even when these ministers are not assigned to the pastoral team, persons involved with Patchwork will call on them to help with personal problems, hospital visitation, and the various rituals (weddings, funerals) of church life.

Sojourners and Messiah have developed the most extensive structures for personal nurture. Their association with Church of the Redeemer influenced their commitment to this aspect of communal life. Redeemer's emphasis on the pastoral needs of community and its success as a fellowship impressed Sojourners and Messiah to implement a process that concentrated on each member's sense of inner wholeness.

At Sojourners, every member had a spiritual director who helped interpret the individual's spiritual journey. Initially, most directors were members of the fellowship; now members select directors from both within and outside the membership. Sojourners also identified members who demonstrated unusual gifts for counseling and designated them as part of the community's counseling team. These persons were supported by the community to acquire professional training in pastoral counseling. They maintained a busy schedule of counseling members who had emotional problems or needed reconciliation in marriage or other relationships. Now Sojourners relies more on a small-group structure (four to six persons) to process personal and interpersonal concerns.

Messiah's structures of nurture were similarly divided. The community organized into small groups that focused on the spiritual growth of members. A counseling team was developed to help members with emotional difficulties. The team's history of training revealed Messiah's dedication to becoming competent with the responsibility of pastoral care. Team members traveled considerable distances to seminars, and counseling trainers were brought to Messiah to conduct workshops. The team devoted several hours per week to group study and the supervised practice of counseling.

They studied New Life Counseling (a method of counseling with prayer), the clinical counseling methods of Frank Lake (blending theological insights with psychological theory), gestalt, transactional analysis, neurolinguistic programming, and divine healing. The methods ranged from individual to group counseling. This training represented a substantial investment of time and money. It indicated how crucial counseling, performed by community members for community members, was to Messiah's fellowship.[4]

Except for Messiah, the demands of living communally led these religious fellowships to feel justified in limiting their therapeutic role. When members of the four other communities were asked about dealing with people with deep emotional problems, the responses most frequently given were these: "This is not a place to come to find oneself." "Community is not designed to provide therapy." "Persons who join community to develop a dependency relationship with others should not be here." "These intentional communities are not for everyone."

Community is a place to be known and loved, and therefore a place to experience the healing power of intimacy. However, it is not a place to "find oneself." One's sense of religious vocation must be clear *before* joining a community. Out of this vocational commitment, one continues in self-discovery and in a deeper understanding of the vocation to which one is called. But the conviction of one's religious vocation must be clear if it is to contribute to the life of an intentional fellowship.

These same communities go the second and third mile to help a member, or even nonmembers closely related to the fellowship, with emotional problems. The support given persons in crisis is extraordinary. Still, they are reluctant to accept new persons into their communal life whose need for therapy is severe enough to exhaust the emotional and physical energies of members. This reluctance is out of concern for those who need help beyond the community's abilities and resources. It also helps the community not be diverted from its mission of social transformation.

When I visited the communities, the pace of life seemed to move between hectic and frantic. Members were extremely busy addressing fellowship and social ministry demands. These communities were not places of retreat. A former Sojourners' member felt that the community would not approve of members taking a day off to just reflect on their spiritual journey; this would be a luxury the community could not afford. While Sojourners' members continue to maintain busy schedules, in recent years they have given themselves the freedom to have more rhythms of rest and retreat.

Another perspective on the work ethic comes from the Koinonia member who said, "Our work is our worship." Work does not inhibit the spiritual quest but is itself a spiritual activity. Personal and interpersonal issues are not abandoned when members are engaged in their work, but their work can become a means to address these concerns.

Some members will complain that such a perspective fails to take seriously the *focused* time and energy required for interpersonal and personal needs. They want the fellowship to be as intentional about relational issues as it is about organizational and social issues. The community must maintain the importance of individuals, not only as contributors to communal work, but as the focus of communal work.

All five communities rely heavily on members being sensitive to each other's emotional needs. This is an act of Christian caring which need not be endorsed through some communal procedure. But all friendships in community are not relationships that can provide mutual aid for emotional crises. A friend may care but not have the skills to counsel. This makes personal and interpersonal care structures important; they are a sign and resource to members who hunger for personal guidance in their spiritual and emotional life.

Communities face the possibility that by developing nurture structures, an inordinate amount of attention will be given to the endless demand of psychological and spiritual problems—thus threatening the commitment to outreach. The other side, however, is that unless a sufficient number of members feel personally whole and perceive the community as a supportive environment, a fellowship will not be energized to implement its mission programs.

For Better, For Worse

We do not fully understand the most significant commitments of our lives when we first make them. At the time of our baptism, we do not anticipate the adversities that will exhaust and fuel our spiritual enthusiasm. Couples vow lifelong marriage unaware of crises that will besiege their relationship. Parents hold their newborn child without knowing the demands this new life will make on them in coming years. Understanding emerges as the uncertain future brings the trials and joys that clarify the true meaning of a past commitment. This also applies to the commitment of community members to live in covenant. Members seek and join community without guarantees of harmony and nurture.

Although members do not have guarantees, they do have strong expectations that community will sustain their religious commitment and personal growth. These expectations are captured in the members' use of the metaphor "family." This is the image most frequently used to describe how intimacy and steadfast commitment to one another characterize covenantal relationships.[5]

The realities of these communities do correspond with fundamental realities of families. As in families, community life can be oppressive as well as liberating, abusive as well as nurturing, judgmental as well as affirming, depressing as well as inspiring. When members use the metaphor, however, they usually refer to the positive qualities of "family." The extent to which a community approximates the more positive meanings of family determines whether members conclude this is the appropriate place for their religious vocation.

As the dream of community takes practical form, however, disappointment sets in. Even an uncertain future holds the promise of fantastic possibilities awaiting birth from labor. But when labor produces a child that is quite ordinary or disappointing, reality is altered. A member of Patchwork, lamenting the increasing frustration that seemed to develop over time, said, "In the early days, everything was clearer." Members are faced with the challenge of accepting communal realities and sustaining enthusiasm for living in covenant.

The anticipation that a community will be the most promising place to experience the fulfillment of being totally committed to God contributes to disappointment. Even when persons have spent time with a particular fellowship before joining, idealism about covenantal living remains. Community is envisioned as having less conflict or more support than actually exists. Members will also misjudge their own abilities to adjust to communal realities. Interdependent living, adopting a simple lifestyle, or living in the community's neighborhood may be appealing disciplines until they stretch the member beyond familiar comfort zones. Persons then discover that, while the community continues to embody their ideals, they overestimated their own ability to live in or to be nurtured by the disciplines of covenantal fellowship.

Disappointment occurs when members have personal commitments not acknowledged by the community as crucial to its life. A member may have an interest in art, but the community does not see how art is useful to its purposes. Or a member might find considerable resistance to using computer technology to assist community projects. Persons become frustrated and feel rejected when the community does not embrace their interests and talents.

A former member of Sojourners found the community to have people with strong and clear commitments. Their agenda would become the order of the day. She concluded that if someone wanted to have a fulfilling experience in the community, they had better "know their gifts and fight like hell for them."

Communities have multiple commitments to their mission and internal life. Any one of these can make a member uneasy about participation in the fellowship. An individual may have primarily joined because of the rich devotional life of the community but now finds she is expected to be involved in the neighborhood ministries that cause her anxiety. Or a member may resent that he is never chosen for leadership roles. Or the religious language of a community may be foreign and even objectionable to a member.

Considering the total life of a community, discontent with one or two areas of its life might seem inconsequential. But the areas of discontent can be emblems of profound differences. The woman who resists involvement in neighborhood ministries also resents that more community time and energy is not given to her personal needs. She dislikes the requirement of living in the neighborhood. And to her dismay, the community's devotional life seems increasingly to emphasize prophetic action while ignoring personal piety.

The man never chosen for leadership recognizes a communal hierarchy that favors longtime members. He believes decision-making cliques have formed based on tenure in the community. In addition to feeling that his leadership abilities are wasted, he believes the deference given to "old-timers" establishes an elite group, jeopardizing the integrity of being in fellowship with companions. These factors of disillusionment and disagreement cause persons to terminate their relationship with communities.

Another major reason for termination relates to the life stages of members rather than to conflict with the community. Members realize that their immediate and long-term needs require them to leave community. One member stated that she had just turned thirty and had never taken control of her life. She now believed that leaving community would enable her to be more independent and responsible. Another member wanted to pursue graduate school and develop a career in a field inspired by his work in the community. Families concerned about the education of their children moved to another part of town or a city with better public schools.

When people leave community because they are making transitions in their own life that cannot be accommodated by the community, their leave-taking need not imply failure of the community. In fact, the clarification of abilities, goals, and needs often results from a fulfilling experience with covenantal relationship. Members then decide their commitment can best be fulfilled by leaving their community and becoming involved in a social service agency, another community, or even the institutional church. For some persons, the call to community may only be for a season of labor and discernment.

Those who remain in the community have mixed reactions to the notion of others being called to community for a "season." Sometimes a person's decision to leave is treated as a sending forth. The community is able to claim its role in preparing the person to honor the religious vocation in a new context. But there are times when an individual's transitions seem to negate the primacy of community over personal and family aspirations. The community feels used as an experiment or adventure rather than a place for long-term commitment.

The hard reality is this: a substantial portion of each community is members unsure of their ongoing commitment to the community. When questioned, they may not have immediate plans to leave, but they foresee the possibility of doing so in the next two or three years. Communities know that the initial commitment to membership needs to be reaffirmed or revised continually. Koinonia, Patchwork, and Sojourners require each member to make an annual assessment of his/her commitment to covenantal living. Acknowledging that every member is in transition, this procedure seeks to renew members' commitment to the community. The communities do not take commitment for granted.

Moreover, not only the members but also the communities themselves are always in transition. The communities' need for revised structures of order, a greater emphasis on art and music, more attention to spiritual formation, the advance of technology, and other transformations of communal life are assessed continually. Intentionality requires that communities examine past commitments in light of current realities. They must update how God's call to community takes a new shape as the uncertain future becomes present certainties.

As stated, the primary indicator of communal well-being is that members feel their covenantal fellowship approximates the qualities of a caring family. Financial hardship and failures in mission efforts will be the occasion for creative solutions and increased resolve. They do not break the spirit of a community nor end its existence. But loss of mutual respect and steadfast caring strikes a deathblow at the very heart of a community.

The prevailing sense of family is not always easy for these communities to determine. The division of labor which pleases some members is the very issue which oppresses others. Or intense interpersonal therapy may be cherished as the community's genius by some and resisted as unnecessary and humiliating by others. Members can have opposing reactions to the same communal realities.

Communities survive and thrive when able to create a fellowship not dependent upon conformity, but which encourages members to remain enthusiastically involved even when they disagree with decisions. While decision making may not always reflect a member's commitment, it must indicate that the member's ideas have been heard and respected. Although feedback on one's character may be critical, the spirit of such feedback must be supportive rather than judgmental.

Life in community is never all good or bad—it is life, with the full range of joys and frustrations. Intentional community, however, tends to accentuate conflicts that might ordinarily be overlooked in the local congregation. The interrelatedness of communal life causes a decision about one matter to have an impact on most other realities of communal life. Members with a clearer sense of their commitment will resist a perceived shift away from that commitment.

The sacrifices people have made to join a community raise the stakes regarding their willingness to tolerate a disagreeable change. Communities must therefore address intense feelings about the quality of covenantal living without fragmenting the fellowship. This is accomplished when members accept deep struggles as necessary and healthy.

Intense intentional community is only possible when a sufficient number of members persevere through the turmoil that is part of sustaining community. They must believe that community is worth the struggle, and that continuing in relationship is more promising than leaving. This is not merely persisting because one believes that a community's eschaton of happiness is near. It is giving oneself to a fellowship because community is the means through which religious vocation is fulfilled.

A Sojourners member said to me, "I've been in this community for fourteen years. Like marriage, it doesn't get any easier. In fact, the last year was perhaps the hardest." The marriage (family) analogy is helpful in understanding covenantal union through difficult times. And like marriage, when the bond of love is evident the relationship can withstand devastating onslaughts of misunderstanding and crises. But without the bond, seemingly inconsequential differences can end relationships. When asked about the most fulfilling experiences of living in their communities, most members responded, "The relationships with other members." When asked about the most frustrating experiences of community, they said, "The relationships with other members." These five communities have kept going through vital expansion and debilitating losses because they have found ways to maintain members who understand that living in covenant is for better and for worse.

To the Glory of God

The desire to live in covenant could be explained through psychological and sociological interpretations. The background of members could be analyzed for influences that led them to seek a covenant fellowship. Interpretations could explore if covenantal living is an effort to compensate for deficiencies in one's experience of family, or if the involvement with social issues is a reaction to a sheltered existence.

This type of analysis can prove insightful. However, while members may be influenced by a multitude of socio-psychological factors, their primary motivation is to participate in a fellowship that empowers them to glorify God.

The residential and economic structures of a community are more than efforts to sustain a communal lifestyle. The structures represent the commitment to organize group life so the community honors God's call upon it. Extended households and residency in the community's neighborhood of mission are covenantal arrangements demonstrating the theological conviction that love requires proximity. Presence is requisite to understanding and care. The theological doctrine of God's presence informs this conviction. God's nearness reassures us that God exercises power with compassion and is not indifferent to our needs and fears.

Living a simple lifestyle not only defines members' relationship to property, but in a profound sense exemplifies members' covenant with one another, neighbors, and God. Jesus' assertion that "You cannot serve God and mammon" (Matt. 6:24) indicates how seriously materialism competes for our loyalty. Mammon becomes an idol we worship in hopes of satisfying our anxiety and greed.

Jesus' words to "not lay up for yourselves treasures on earth, where moth and rust consume and where thieves break in and steal" (Matt. 6:19) may only convince us to moth-proof, insure, and double the guard over our treasures. Simplicity for these communities is a discipline of resistance against such idolatry. It is also a lifestyle that conserves resources, therefore enabling one to exercise responsible stewardship upon God's earth.

Proximity, interdependence, simplicity, and social transformation are religious convictions that, when demonstrated in a community's life, become visible signs of a fellowship's devotion to God. However, the most revealing sign of a community's religious orientation is its worship.

When first contacted for this study, each community insisted that attendance at its worship services was essential to understanding the community. I found this insistence to be true. Worship was a time I experienced the religious enthusiasm that fuels covenantal commitment.

The services were characterized by participatory liturgies, lively congregational singing, and verbal congregational response to the various liturgical acts of worship. Informality prevailed. Most persons wore casual clothes and interacted with fellow worshipers in a relaxed mood. Requests for intercessory prayer, a warm and personal welcoming of visitors, and hugs were features of worship in all of the communities. Worship seemed designed and conducted to encourage intimacy with one another and with God. Sermons, prayers, and announcements revealed prophetic commitment; peace and justice issues were proclaimed as God's agenda.

Worship defined community identity and purpose, and it inspired discipleship. This involved more than extolling the merits of living in community. It was a celebration of God's presence and love. Consequently, in some of the communities, worship attracted more nonmembers than members. People were drawn to the vitality of the services and felt energized for their spiritual journey. They cherished this time of communal life without feeling the necessity to become members of the community. The centrality of God to the community's sense of itself and its work was evident.

While the content of worship reveals much about a community's theology, useful insights come from examining the timing and context of worship. Members of Patchwork and Koinonia attend the Sunday morning services and join churches in their vicinity.

Sunday evenings the two communities have their own worship services, which are open to anyone. The evening services often reflect the members' sensitivities to communal concerns and their creative approach to religious celebration. Instead of choosing a communal worship time which competes with the services of local churches, this scheduling allows members to join in devotion and fellowship with neighbors. It is an assertion of oneness with the Christians and churches of their vicinity.

Koinonia periodically invites guest preachers and their congregations to participate in their services. The invitation reaffirms Koinonia's desire to be in close fellowship with neighbors and places neighbors in the role of nurturing the community's spiritual growth.

Patchwork experiments with innovative liturgies that emphasize the arts and congregational involvement in liturgy. These services attract persons from the Evansville area who find Patchwork's worship and fellowship invaluable to their spiritual needs. The community receives significant support for its ministries from persons involved in these evening services.

Messiah and Voice of Calvary hold their worship services on Sunday morning. They are developing their own churches as the primary locus of worship for their members and others. Covenantal fellowship and church are one. Until 1991, Sojourners also held worship services on Sunday morning. The worship time was changed to Sunday evenings to allow members to experience the Sunday morning worship and fellowship of neighborhood churches. Still, Sojourners own worship service has continued to be the primary context of worship for its members.

The religious experience in worship sometimes is the primary reason members remain with a community through debilitating conflict and stress. Worship revitalizes. Even when problems
do not subside, worship renews members and renews their
commitment. As Carlyle Marney, minister and author, so aptly
states, "The antidote to exhaustion is not rest, but worship."[6] The
power experienced in worship is the power that sustains these
communities when times are for better and for worse.

This does not mean, however, that worship assures membership retention. The focus of worship is God. The decision to
leave community can be understood as the fulfillment of one's
commitment to God. The ultimate commitment a person makes
is to respond to God's will. Community may be understood as
the context in which the commitment to God is fulfilled, but
community should not be confused with the commitment itself.

Howard Thurman speaks of the religious person's tempta-
tion "to make an idol of commitment."[7] Rather than exercising a
commitment to God, one has a commitment to a commitment.
All openness to God's leading becomes secondary to the commitment to a particular career or place or fellowship. Seeking
and leaving community can be actions to glorify God.

Worship, in all of the communities, expresses a religious vitality that draws members and nonmembers into closer fellowship. Because it is rooted in God, worship centers on the one
who is of all. A community plans worship but does not control
its impact. And while worship expresses the heart of communal
commitment, its effect transforms and transcends the community. Like social outreach, worship widens the community's circle
of intimacy as well as energizes and renews the commitment to
justice. Consequently worship helps communities never to be
complacent about nor live under the delusion that they have
achieved perfect intimacy and mission in their covenantal living.

For the Church Today

The challenging question for every church is this: Does this fellowship with companions, for better or for worse, help clarify
and empower members' discipleship as they seek to respond to

God's call upon their lives? In answering this question, it is important to do more than assess the leadership capabilities of laity or ordained clergy. The question requires a congregation to determine if its fellowship cultivates members' sense of Christian identity and mission where members are known and loved. Thomas E. Frank criticizes churches' emphasis upon persuasive intellectual appeals about faith while neglecting the significance of belonging to a fellowship of faith.

> George Gallup has shown that well over 60% of North Americans do not consider church membership necessary for Christian life or faith. So modern theology has gotten the church it deserves: a voluntary association composed of solitary individuals who participate only if it meets their personal needs or strengthens the intellectual arguments that will make faith claims plausible. And if one is satisfied and feels no particular need, why participate? Over 90% of North Americans say they believe in a higher being anyway.[8]

Frank's criticism accurately links Christian nurture and witness to a fellowship of faith. Christian discipleship is dependent upon where one *belongs* in addition to what one believes.

Church membership is more than completing a ritual of joining, attending church activities, and giving financial support. These can be done without a significant personal commitment to the congregation—a commitment which entrusts the congregation with shaping religious identity and service, and a commitment which contributes to the congregation's faithfulness to God. Church membership is the acceptance of and participation in a covenant with others who seek to glorify God through worship, study, and service.

An important feature of this covenant is the understanding that members are *in fellowship with companions*. A sense of common purpose that defines identity and commitment characterizes togetherness. As discussed earlier, this sense of common purpose is strong among the religious communities. Members leave jobs, move great distances, relinquish wealth, and adopt the disciplines of the communities' order because they are inspired by the *focused* commitment of the fellowship.

Members of local congregations are often involved with their churches for very different reasons. Denominational identity, family history with a congregation, opportunities to interact with persons of one's own racial, economic, and social group, or geographical convenience might be primary reasons for members belonging. In such circumstances, a congregation's sense of purpose may be veiled or absent because purpose is not central to determining membership.

This is not to demean the importance of denomination, family, social comfort, or geography as aspects of membership; these powerful factors contribute to membership loyalty and enthusiasm. However, Christian discipleship is best discerned in a context where the mission of the church determines the reason for belonging. A common passion to respond to God's calling should be the basis of members' sense of being in fellowship with companions.

Some churches have a statement of covenantal fellowship that is the result of their denomination's deliberations. Congregations will also create statements that reflect their local membership's understanding of the mission of the church.

When a congregation has a covenant, several questions arise about the function of the covenant in empowering the fellowship. Is the covenant displayed where it is regularly seen by members? How is the covenant reaffirmed? Does everyone have the same interpretation of the covenant's meaning? If not, how does the congregation discern the meaning of the covenant for decision making about the fellowship? Does the covenant adequately define the meaning of belonging to the particular fellowship? Does the covenant help the congregation to be intentional in its worship, programs, and expenditures? What changes would the members and the church have to make if the covenant was to be taken seriously? What difference would it make in the way the church functions if there was no covenant? In answering such questions, the power or impotence of a church's covenant to guide the formation and work of the church becomes evident.

Many churches do not have a written covenant. These congregations might ascertain whether there is an unwritten yet operative covenant that shapes their fellowship. Many of the above questions could then be applied after this unwritten covenant is defined.

Congregations sometimes suffer from covenantal amnesia. They have a loss of memory about past commitments members made to one another as companions of the fellowship. Members' feelings that the congregation used to be more like a family may reflect changes in membership or a shift in the centrality of the church to members' lives. But these feelings can also result when the covenant which strengthened their caring bond fades from consciousness.

Retrieving the history of commitment and care could be an important starting point for assessing the present state of covenantal relationships in the congregation. A congregation might then initiate the process of writing a covenant that reflects members' current beliefs about the mission of their church and the meaning of membership.

The strongest sense of purpose, mutual care, cooperation, and commitment occur within covenantal relationship— whether such a covenant is written or not. Relationships of trust depend on covenant. Cooperative action to realize common beliefs relies on a sense of covenant that entails expectations of responsibility and accountability.

The hunger *to be known and loved* expressed by members of these religious communities is also a hunger of persons in congregations. Intimacy is integral to being a companion with another. The term *companion* literally means one with whom bread is eaten. The significance of this term becomes manifest after one realizes that throughout the world eating together in public is a bold assertion of intimacy. People who choose to sleep together will not necessarily be seen in public eating together. To be at table breaking bread, whether in a restaurant or in a church for holy communion, is a public witness of intimate relationship.

Covenant without intimacy is vapid, stiff, and procedural. A congregation may begin as a gathering of strangers, but soon the expectation for intimacy persists. Churches, like religious communities, use the metaphor "family" to identify what members ought to be for one another. And the quality of fellowship in churches, as in religious communities, is frequently based on their ability to approximate images of care and understanding associated with loving families.

Churches use their worship services to engender intimacy among members. The liturgy's "prayers of the people" will invite persons to voice their concerns and requests for prayer before the congregation. Passing the peace can be a time of greeting and embracing. Announcements inform about the achievements, celebrations, and needs of members. The time and structure of worship, however, limit the extent to which persons can tarry with one another's concerns. Churches therefore seek to foster intimacy by creating small groups where members can be known and loved. Intimacy in a congregation does not mean that each individual is intimate with every member, but that each individual has caring involvement with someone or a group of members.

These smaller gatherings are sometimes called care groups, nurture groups, birthday clubs, prayer fellowships, covenant groups, and other names that suggest a supportive fellowship. Or a church will form groups around particular life issues of members: divorce, being a single adult, addiction, grief, physical disabilities, aging. And churches will orient their regular organizations such as Sunday school classes, Bible study meetings, youth groups, and choir fellowship to address the intimacy needs of members. Small groups become therapeutic structures where companions experience covenant as intimacy.

Intimacy without covenant is experimental, self-indulging, and perhaps exploitative. The relationship has no higher significance than the information and feelings that emerge from intimacy. Confidential disclosures of members' foibles are not taken as opportunities for bearing one another's burdens and healing. Rather, condemnation and gossip ensues. Vulnerability then becomes the occasion for oppression rather than care and freedom. If the church group still thinks of itself as a family, without covenant, members are likely to consider the family as abusive and dysfunctional.

Smaller groups, where the most private concerns are revealed to others, run the danger of having participants who violate the covenant of confidentiality or who lack the skills to help those in need. Pastors also need to recognize how covenant functions in their pastoral care relationships. Persons are injured when their pastor shares data from a private counseling session as a sermon illustration. True intimacy requires covenant.

Members of local congregations are not church-dependent for addressing their intimacy needs. Members experience intimacy possibilities through involvement with family, colleagues, recreation teams, and other interactive settings. No expectation may exist for their church to be a place of intimacy.

The availability of multiple contexts of intimacy in the larger society is to be valued by the church. But the church should not relinquish or abdicate the necessity of establishing contexts of intimacy within itself. If the church is a place where members are in fellowship with companions, there remains the need to be known and loved by fellow members who share the commitment to Christian discipleship.

While intimacy may surface on the job or with friends, the empowerment of Christian discipleship is not the primary goal of these contexts. The church, however, is called to be a fellowship totally committed to increasing understanding and deepening relationships that empower Christian discipleship. The absence of intimacy in a congregation may impair its ability to nurture members in understanding the meaning of covenant in a Christian fellowship and in the Christian faith.

Paul wrote to the church at Corinth about a variety of spiritual gifts deserving appreciation. He then instructs the church

> Love is patient and kind; love is not jealous or boastful; it is not arrogant or rude. Love does not insist on its own way; it is not irritable or resentful; it does not rejoice at wrong, but rejoices in the right. Love bears all things, believes all things, hopes all things, endures all things. (1 Cor. 13:4-7)

This continues to be a message to the church today. Although we seek to practice love wherever we are related with others, we have an increased expectation to experience this reality of love in the church. The church is a community called to exemplify this truth it professes.

A congregation should identify where in the church's schedule and structure members experience the love of church companions bearing their burdens. A church should assess if and how its ministries help members in understanding and honoring the covenantal dimensions of intimacy. Congregations need to be places where members can bring "all things" with the assurance of being embraced by love.

Crucial to this covenant of companionship and intimacy is the commitment to others *for better and for worse*. Or as Paul says, love "endures all things." Congregational life dependent on harmony or conflict fails to honor the commitment to relationship regardless of circumstance. We live in a society that values mobility as a way to remedy dissatisfaction. We move to better neighborhoods rather than work to improve the ones in which we live. We buy our way into private education or purchase homes in better school districts rather than improve the quality of local public schools.

Some social observers have attributed a high number of divorces to the longing of persons to "trade up" to a better quality of spouse. Even church loyalty will sometimes seem contingent on a church's ability to meet the "religious product" demands of members as consumers.

This urge to move on when relationships are disappointing is not only caused by fickleness, but by a deficiency of the spirit to remain steadfast with another. William F. May considers this problem a "deadness of soul." It is a boredom one feels when an object of affection no longer stimulates and excites. A person tends to lament that the object has failed him or her, when actually this is the result of an interior inadequacy. May concludes that this not only applies to relationships with other persons, but also with God. He says, "In boredom before God, it is man who has failed his object, and not the reverse . . . the man of faith must confess his boredom as his sin because his attitude reflects the poverty of his own soul."[9] Boredom, disappointment, and frustration may be cause for self-examination rather than the termination of relationship.

Despite the importance of perseverance, termination of some relationships, such as those in which abuse is present, is appropriate. Separation can be a creative response to situations where there is little possibility to transform destructive interactions. Loyalty relies upon companionship and caring. If the covenant is already broken by abuse, then leaving the relationship is not a matter of being unfaithful. Love enduring all things does not mean that persons are required to submit themselves to abuse. Some form of reconciliation after the abuse has ended may be the most fitting act of endurance.

We can make an idol of maintaining relationship. Even intimacy and mission can become golden calves. To live in covenant is not to idolize the covenant's features of companionship, intimacy, and steadfast faithfulness. Covenant is made *to the glory of God*. Covenant is instrumental to fulfilling God's call upon the church. The agenda for the church, therefore, is to establish covenantal relationships among members to glorify God by the love made manifest in its fellowship and witness to the world.

We also idolize traditions that frequently weaken the bond of covenant. Congregations need to be receptive to creating new organizational structures that involve members who feel on the periphery of church life, yet who wish to contribute to decision making that guides their fellowship. Gender inclusive language during worship can spawn an atmosphere where the full fellowship finally feels acknowledged as faith is articulated in word and song. Multicultural sources for music can introduce a new awareness of God. These types of changes may threaten congregational traditions—traditions which some members have a deep investment in maintaining.

The challenge before congregations is to honor the covenant of companionship and intimacy, even when such honoring means the transformation of traditions and structures. Discipleship is cultivated by community, and community is sustained by covenant. Congregations alive to the discipleship needs of members are alive to God's call to fellowship and covenant. They are therefore alive to God—who knows and loves them, for better and for worse.

CHAPTER 4

Creating a Holy Order

By What Authority?

The call to community heralds a new vision of vocation. While adherents are absorbed in the ecstasy of being called, this question soon emerges: How does vision become reality? Strategies and methods must be devised to translate ideals into practice. Eventually a form of organization must be created to implement the call. Loyalty and energy need to be focused if the demands of the call are to be met.

Passive submission to a megalomaniac who requires mindless obedience is a popular stereotype about religious communalism. Contrary to this stereotype, authority and compliance in the five communities this book examines function under democratic procedures. Active submission to the authority *of the community* is the fundamental principle which orders group life.

This principle recognizes the interdependent nature of personal growth. The individual is dependent on others for guidance and must submit to their decisions. The self is not extinguished nor swallowed up by a group, but a proper sense of self emerges when it acknowledges authority to which it submits. All the while the individual retains the right to challenge and reject the claim of such authority over specific decisions felt to violate covenantal living. Submission is freedom from the enslavement of self-deception, self-righteousness, and self-indulgence.

Stressing the importance of submission to authority often creates a wary response. Submission is so strongly linked with situations of abuse that it is discarded as leading to destructive rather than constructive relationships. Counselors attest to the anguish of battered women who have remained in abusive households because they have tried to be faithful to the Scripture's admonition.

> Wives, submit to your own husbands, as to the Lord. For the husband is head of the wife, as also Christ is head of the church; and He is the Savior of the body. Therefore, just as the church is subject to Christ, so let the wives be to their own husbands in everything. (Eph. 5:22-24, NKJV)

Although the passage was never intended as license for abuse, incidents of battering reinforce suspicions that submission leads to negative consequences. Images of despotic rule in families, cults, and national governments come forth when submission is touted as a discipline.

Submission in covenantal relationship involves the understanding that authority cares about the welfare of each member of the covenant. The authority seeks to help a member fulfill a calling the member has already agreed to. Persons in authority do not create or impose the calling. The authorities profess to have a common calling with those who submit.

Within the communities, submission means the individual acknowledges an identity defined within the context of the group. Individual identities then help define the group identity. Submission is commitment to the group and the processes that strengthen group identity and solidarity. Members entrust their lives to a fellowship for which they accept responsibility. Participating in and abiding by the decision making structures and rules of communal life are crucial ways submission is practiced.

All members are expected to provide direction to communal life. As deliberation moves to decision making, members seek to form a consensus. Arriving at consensus does not mean that a religious community has received enthusiastic agreement from 100 percent of its membership. Achieving consensus means that the process of deliberation has encouraged all persons to discuss thoroughly the issue. Even though some members may not favor a proposal, they are willing to accept (and usually to actively help implement) the proposal as a commitment of the community. However, when the adamant dissent of a few is not mollified, consensus is not reached and the community is prevented from enacting ideas that have majority support.

This indicates a deep respect for the concerns and contributions of each member. It also suggests how important the participatory process is to communal order and decisions of commitment. The democratic process is conducted almost to a fault. An interminable amount of time may pass before a community can satisfy members' reservations about a change in procedure or the implementation of a new program. Communities form a multitude of committees so that members can thoroughly evaluate and discuss aspects of communal life. At one time, for example, Sojourners had thirty-one members assigned to twenty-nine committees.

The emergence of committees as a dominant structure within communal organization means members give more time and energy to the administration of the community. Communal involvement becomes increasingly bureaucratic. But members eventually become weary of meetings that generate more committees and more meetings. Over time, communities realize that bureaucratization is a problem and try to streamline unwieldy decision-making structures.

But this streamlining is not pursued at the expense of taking away members' responsibility for the guidance of their fellowship. Communities are sensitive to the charge, and resistant to the possibility, of being governed by autocratic leadership. This is evident in Sojourners' 1971 self-description. "We are a chiefless movement. . . ." As the community matured, views of leadership roles became more positive, and members asserted that "leaders should help build consensus rather than make decisions for the group."

Early in its history Koinonia also struggled with leadership issues. As Dallas Lee, the community's biographer, expressed it, "No one wanted to be in the position of lording it over the others, and they all expressed a reluctance at being 'officers.' " Whoever had the responsibility for coordinating work assignments was referred to as the "dictator" and was "dis-elected" after a brief tenure.[1]

Lee also noted that a tragedy of Koinonia's history was that its phobia toward assertive leadership kept it from taking full advantage of Clarence Jordan's biblical scholarship. Jordan was reticent to assert his authority in any way that might suggest a superior knowledge or role in the fellowship. Members also resented his many outside speaking engagements, because they speculated that these invitations prevented Jordan from participating in Koinonia's life as an "ordinary" member.

Today Koinonia is more comfortable with individuals taking major responsibility for facets of communal life. Decisions are primarily made by committees, but the community assigns areas of responsibility and authority to members without being paranoid about the possibilities for authoritarian rule.

The founders of Patchwork Central were concerned about authoritarian rule and the possibility that a hierarchy of membership responsibilities would develop. Their concerns were reflected in their statement on community governance which stressed the need for "shared" and "horizontal" leadership. Leadership positions were to rotate among members every twelve months. Patchwork's egalitarian model was based on the belief that all members were capable of performing the varied responsibilities of communal governance.

This conviction is especially understandable since Patchwork's small membership was made up of persons well-educated in group leadership. The model affirmed the abilities of the members. Each member, by virtue of his or her sense of calling and the leadership structure, had opportunity to determine the shape of covenantal living. If the community had been larger, with a broader range of leadership abilities, the wisdom of such a model would have been suspect.

Patchwork placed tremendous emphasis on valuing the individual. As mentioned, even its name symbolized the significance of unique patches of material which together made a beautiful and useful quilt. So while members submitted to a communal identity and purpose, Patchwork (more than the other four communities) stressed the importance of the community devoting itself to the identity and calling of each member. The community would focus on the particular interests of a member (even if other members were initially unenthusiastic about those interests). They affirmed the member and their covenant of mutual support by giving the member's project their time, energy, and financial resources.

Although Voice of Calvary asserted the importance of consensus decision making, its procedures and perspective on leadership were different than the other communities. From the inception, John Perkins aggressively defined what the community should be. His approach was consistent with the traditional leadership role of black ministers, who are expected to be visionaries and set the direction of their churches. Perkins did this at VOCM. His strong convictions often determined what the community would tackle, even if VOCM's Board of Directors and other staff members had not been consulted.

Lem Tucker, Perkins' successor as president of VOCM, had a more managerial than charismatic/visionary style of leadership. His consultative approach tended to give staff and board a greater influence over VOCM's direction. Still, VOCM functioned under a more hierarchical model than the other communities. In addition to the black church tradition, the hierarchical approach was conducive to VOCM's methods of mission, which drew heavily on a business administration model for delivering services to their constituents.

The VOC Fellowship is led by elders and a pastoral team of three clergy (one of whom is salaried). They guide the church's programs and attend to pastoral needs of members. This structure resembles the authority and responsibilities given pastors and administrative boards of local congregations.

A major authority issue for VOCM and VOCF is the role one plays in determining the identity of the other. John Perkins founded them with the expectation that they would function as two expressions of a single commitment. The Ministries would enable staff and volunteers to experience the empowering of poor black people by addressing such basic needs as housing, economic development, health care, and education. The Fellowship would be the religious gathering that focused on inspiring worship, Christian education, intimate gatherings of caring, and outreach to the immediate West Jackson area.

The melding of these two organizations continues to be an ongoing matter of tension. The executive directors of VOCM have been elders in the VOCF. And the salaried pastor of VOCF has served on the board of VOCM. Fellowship members have been apprised of the work of the Ministries and encouraged to support this work. At one time it was expected that VOCM staff would belong to VOCF and live in the area of mission. But recently not all Ministries staff have been required to become members of the Fellowship and live in West Jackson.

While each organization has a definite structure of authority, members of both organizations feel unsure about the authoritative bond that unites them. The bond used to be the authority of John Perkins. Some VOCF staff and members believe that Perkins' founding image should continue to be the authoritative bond.

But the declaration of organizational autonomy (which both the Ministries and Fellowship make) complicates the affirmation of a singular witness. Occasions do arise when the perceived staff needs of the Ministries conflict with the membership and residency expectations of the Fellowship. No individual nor decision-making group has the authority to force one organization to yield to the desires of the other.

All five communities are aware that a community's vital commitment can be immobilized in a quagmire of diverse opinions. Consequently, the principle of submission is essential to the fulfillment of a community's calling. Submission of the individual to the will of the community and to those with designated authority is basic for members to acquire a communal identity that transcends individual prerogative. Persons are not being asked to abandon their God-given powers of evaluation and free agency. But they are urged to participate in and trust the process of communal discernment and to risk the possibility of error with the community. This is the only way a communal identity can be developed and preserved.

Sojourners, Voice of Calvary Fellowship, and Messiah have elders who oversee the various activities of their respective communities. At Koinonia, this group is called the "fellowship team." Patchwork's community life is currently directed by a management team that addresses administrative and programmatic issues and a pastoral team that focuses upon personal concerns and interpersonal conflict.

Those with oversight responsibilities in the five communities are confirmed by the total membership. They are chosen for their demonstrated sensitivities to the pulse of the community (especially in matters of pastoral care and the quality of group life), and for their gifts to structure proposals that resolve members' problems. Even when a community's organization has delegated authority, it is understood that the total membership retains control over the decision-making process.

Just as communities recognize the threat of individualism and authoritarian rule, they are also leery of being distracted from their calling by nonmembers' sense of priorities. Decisions about the welfare of the fellowship are the sole responsibility of members.

This principle especially applies to matters of intimacy. Times of mutual criticism where members examine each other's personal growth and communal involvement are attended exclusively by members. Even interns who have worked closely with the community may not be invited to such occasions. When nonmembers participate in communal discussions, all matters of communal intimacy are decided by members only.

The communities broaden the base of decision making when determining matters of mission. For example, since 1970 Koinonia has had an incorporated board that directs its ministries and business. Of the board's eleven members, only two are resident partners. This represents a major relinquishing of decision making to persons outside the communal membership. Partners trust the board to direct and enhance their ministries. The board, however, is acutely aware of the partners' opinions and their key role in the success of Koinonia's ministries. Consequently, the board makes decisions which are in accord with the partners' vision of Koinonia's development.

Although Voice of Calvary Ministries Board does not include members of its staff, the board makes decisions in consultation with VOC staff leaders. Patchwork's board used to be selected by the covenant members—all of whom were also board members. Until 1983 the covenant members outnumbered other board participants. Even after the board had a majority of non-members, its decision making reflected a deference to the will of covenant members. The prevailing feeling was that those who made the greatest personal sacrifice to support communal ministries (covenant members) should determine the direction of the organization. Covenant members, however, have increasingly relinquished their influence to Patchwork's board. Currently, of Patchwork's twenty-eight board members, only about a third are covenant members.

Sojourners supported the empowering of poor tenants to run the tenants union it organized and staffed. The Sojourners Neighborhood Center is directed by a board of eleven persons; only three are members of the Sojourners community. The other Sojourners ministries have been directed by the Sojourners membership. Messiah established boards for its neighborhood schools and its housing program that involved people from its neighborhood. The ultimate responsibility for these programs remained with the church.

The communities draw on nonmembers for consultation, volunteer labor, and participation on the boards of specific ministries. Except for the distinctions noted between membership influence and membership control at Koinonia and Patchwork, the power to direct programs initiated by the communities remains with their membership. The authority to guide communal efforts comes with the commitment of membership. Those who have heeded the call to community are reluctant to place in hands of nonmembers the power to determine how the call is fulfilled.

Maintaining Boundaries of Community

Boundaries define community. They help establish place, identity, and meaning. Membership is the most important boundary marker of intentional communities. Membership criteria distinguish a religious community within the larger church and society. Covenantal living is primarily defined by those within the boundary of membership.

Communities recognize this crucial function of membership and therefore work hard to establish appropriate criteria. On the one hand they want an open door for all attracted by the community's vision. Any hint of becoming an exclusive group is repulsive to the communities. Yet if belonging to the fellowship requires specific commitments of time, resources, and a way of life, then the communities feel obligated to be discriminating in membership approval. They need members who will contribute to the group's purposes rather than be a constant source of frustration and complaint.

Koinonia's history illustrates this struggle. It was not until 1951, nine years after its birth, that Koinonia established requirements and a statement of commitment for members. Before then, the only obligation of joiners was to participate in the community's practice of economic sharing.

The new process for membership required joiners to go through three membership stages: *novice* (about three months in which a person participated in communal activities but did not make the economic commitment nor the pledge to fully submit to communal authority); *provisional* (three-nine months in which one studied Scripture to inform and assess forthcoming commitment to full membership); and *full* (all possessions either given away or to the community, with a covenant made to abide by Koinonia's rules and practices).[2]

This more structured procedure was developed in response to serious conflict within the fellowship. Disagreements about raising children, time away from Koinonia, the equity of economic arrangements, and many other procedures of communalism threatened the unity and survival of the community. A written pledge, a time to test the commitment of new adherents, and the insistence that the community be more explicit about each member's obligations were efforts to make individuals more deliberate in deciding to join Koinonia. This membership process, developed out of crisis, has continued with few modifications for over four decades.[3]

Sojourners devised a similar membership process. Seven years after its founding, Sojourners experienced a flood of new members. Many of these persons had no realistic understanding of communal living. Some soon left. Others needed extensive counseling from a core group of members who helped them adjust to community. The dual impact of people leaving and the emotional exhaustion of counseling led Sojourners to develop a protracted membership process. Contrary to potential members' images, community was not a sanctuary from social strife or personal crises. Their frustration with communal realities often erupted into virulent attacks on the integrity of the fellowship.

It is more difficult to address dissatisfactions after a person has become a full member of a community. Members wrestle with each other's problems because this is the nature of the covenant of intimacy. Even when a fellow member is obviously out of harmony with communal purposes, excessive amounts of time and emotional energy will be given to bringing about a resolution. If the community can determine that persons are not suited for membership before they are full-fledged participants in communal life, then their disruptive involvement is limited to the specified period of discernment.

Since Koinonia and Sojourners required members to relinquish their financial assets, and since both also provided financial support to individuals who left their community, clearly it benefited them to decide membership potential before the economic commitment was made. Trying to provide resources so terminated members could reestablish themselves in the larger society was emotionally and fiscally draining for the community. Extensive membership procedures sought to save the joiners and the community from the exasperating arrangements that accompanied termination.

Patchwork Central never had an extensive membership process. The small size of the fellowship caused more anxiety about not having members than about assimilating new ones. When five of the ten covenant members suddenly left, members wondered if their dreams of growth would ever be realized. They doubted so few members could carry the responsibilities of the ministries. The heavy time commitment and unstated expectation to live in the neighborhood of communal ministries were dropped as membership requirements. Consequently, the membership soon tripled, increasing optimism for the community's future.

With Koinonia and Sojourners the welfare of the community was preserved by expanding the requirements for membership. At Patchwork reducing the requirements was perceived as the strategy for survival.

Determining matters of membership at Church of the Messiah was never complicated. The Episcopal Church's membership requirements were the only rules for joining which Messiah could enforce. However by 1978, 100 of Messiah's 170 members participated in the Common Life group, which required the economic commitments and living arrangements previously described. So while Messiah could not technically impose stringent membership requirements on individuals, the communal commitment of the majority of members soon established an unstated but effective standard of *fully committed* participation.

A common criterion for membership in both the Voice of Calvary Ministries and Fellowship was for persons to affirm the VOC "Statement of Faith." The statement asserted biblical inerrancy, Trinitarian doctrine, the virgin birth of Jesus, human depravity, the atoning work of Jesus' crucifixion, and the bodily raising of the dead for divine judgment. Among communities, VOC was the only one to require a dogmatic profession of faith as a prerequisite to membership.

The other communities assert the authority of the Scriptures and the example of Jesus in directing their faith pilgrimage, but they avoid dogmatic affirmation. The statement of faith gives VOC a theological identity that appeals to Christians of a more theologically conservative orientation. It therefore helps clarify who should join VOC.

While all of the communities were open to new members, their requirements for membership reduced the risk of succumbing to chaos and fragmentation because of the influx of joiners. The *process* of membership defined and preserved the communities' identity. Admission procedures disclosed a community's covenant and commitments, and encouraged involvement only from those willing to work on behalf of these commitments through covenantal relationship. Enforcement of the membership criteria reassured the communities that membership growth provided continuity instead of devastating change. As a boundary marker, membership was threatened not only by candidates for membership but also by nonmembers. During a period in Sojourners' and Messiah's life, dating and romantic relationships members had with nonmembers were questioned. The communities felt that their intimacy, organizational, and mission demands did not leave time for a serious member to be involved with nonmembers who could not give themselves to the work of the community. Restrictions against intimacy with nonmember were eventually dropped by these two communities. They realized that relationships with nonmembers relieved stress arising from the intensity of communal living. In addition, regulating relationships felt like an invasion of privacy, distrust of members, and putting members in the role of children needing parental guidance.[4]

Major complications arose in each community from the involvement and influence of nonmembers who supported communal activities but chose not to fulfill requirements for membership. Each community had a core of nonmembers passionate about the community's goals but unwilling to join.

Here we are *not* discussing the volunteers and interns which communities have for an extended period of time. Persons in these categories of support usually understand and accept their restricted role in community life. They have a prescribed time period for their service to the community. Their commitment to labor with the community to fulfill its purposes may be as enduring as those of members. This nonmember core has been indispensable as communities sought to accomplish their mission.[5]

Nonmembers are prominent in the outreach ministries and worship life of communities. Their initial participation in a community will frequently be for purposes of mission. Even the appeal of worship is because of a community's sensitivity to incorporating social concerns within the worship experience. A participant in Patchwork's worship said she preferred the liturgy of her church and she had no intentions of leaving her local congregation; however, she would continue to come to Patchwork's worship services because she believed in the community's witness to individuals and society.

But soon the interests of nonmembers turn to matters of intimacy. The extensive time given to outreach and worship results in close relationships with members. The nonmembers are increasingly drawn to the community as a context for fellowship as well as service. More and more the community becomes the central place of meaning. And members come to appreciate the support group as partners in the community's work and identity.

Nonmembers often become discontent with the distinctions made between them and members. They feel that they have a second-class communal status. With qualms about the criteria of membership as valid marks of commitment, they may challenge the need to live in the community's neighborhood, or economic sharing, or common households as requirements for full participation in communal decision making and fellowship. They may pressure a community to change boundaries of commitment to open all opportunities for communal intimacy to nonmembers.

Nonmembers' desire to restructure the bases of participation in group life could be interpreted as their sense of call to community. They feel compelled to join the communal fellowship and work that embodies their profoundest convictions. Their experiences with the community confirm their belief that the most significant demands for their discipleship can be realized with the community. But they do not believe that restricting economic and living arrangements is necessary.

Communities resist this redefining of membership. The experiences of intimacy and mission are the outgrowth of a communal way of life felt to be inextricable from the structures of order that have shaped communal identity.

These criteria of inclusion raise doubts about the appropriateness of the metaphor "family" to describe a communal fellowship. The effort to have intimate caring relationships with many and diverse people could be compared to an *extended* (as distinct from *nuclear*) family model. Except for the promises and vows of marriage, we usually do not think of belonging to a family as requiring one to declare a new way of life. Being part of a family is often associated with who one *is* (by virtue of birth relationship or marriage) rather than what one believes and does. In these religious communities, a sense of call and covenantal living are the operative bases of relationship.

For example, a spouse of a community member is not automatically "family." The spouse must request admission and demonstrate readiness to live by the disciplines that define the community. The members must decide if the request and demonstration adequately indicate that the spouse will contribute to communal purpose. The spouse may feel like part of the extended family only *after* entry into the community.

Boundary maintenance indicates who belongs and what that belonging means. The boundary is not to distinguish good people from evil people, nor faithful Christians from slack ones. The emphasis on membership criteria identifies the companions one can trust with the call to be a peculiar people in a particular place for an uncertain future.

By Trial and Error and Trial

Order is "holy" because it serves a divine purpose. It transforms religious ideal into religious reality. Disparate ventures and raging enthusiasm are harnessed into a unified commitment. Order puts flesh on the discipline to achieve the promise of word. It enables a body's many members to serve one purpose. Communities invest considerable time and energy in matters of order because they realize this provides the coherence necessary for them to be faithful and effective in fulfilling their call.

Particular structures are not sacred in and of themselves. God has not given an organizational flow chart that guarantees righteousness. Neither is the order itself understood to have the inherent value of goodness because it reflects a divine reality (as in the Shakers' belief that their architecture and furniture imaged God's will for perfected design). The best constructed scheme of organization remains susceptible to all the distortions and foibles of which human nature is capable.

Communal structures are not devised as mechanisms to control behavior or to make life predictable so a utopian social order can be established. While all forms of order enforce conformity and routinize life to some extent, the purpose of order goes beyond creating a controlled environment.

The history of the five communities reveals that routine, procedure, and policy are no panacea to a community's difficulties. Structures of order are as apt to create problems as they are to resolve them. These communities are not formed to make life more organized, but to organize it more intentionally for fulfilling a calling.

The rationale for particular structures of order is similar to the explanation given earlier for a community's call. Structure has *theological warrants* which are based upon biblical models of sharing. Members' decisions about living arrangements, methods of outreach, worship, and pastoral care draw on experiences or ideals from their *personal histories*. And attention has been given to the way *life setting* or context of a community can determine options for housing, worship, and outreach.

The predominant rationale for a particular structure is *pragmatic*. Order is valued for its capacity to mediate effectively and efficiently the members' temperament and their sense of covenant and communal goals. This demand upon order is the main reason these communities make numerous changes in their structures. They do not pretend to establish unchangeable structures of order. Order must be flexible enough to accommodate new sensitivities and situations of communal life. A rigid commitment to order leads to the deterioration of a fellowship. Concern for the welfare of those living under the rules of order rejuvenates a community.

Structures designed for single and childless adults must be redesigned as the community evolves with married couples and children. The rhythm of community meetings and budget allotments must reflect the new reality of families. They must also respond to the members' new interests (such as receiving additional education and training, and increased involvement in neighborhood issues). A community's schedule of gatherings has to be assessed to determine if it facilitates intimacy and mission or weariness and conflict.

The most common form of structural revision is the simplification (or streamlining) of living arrangements, economics, and decision making. Extended households are abandoned in favor of smaller or individual living units. Common treasuries are revised to allow more personal responsibility for one's finances. Decisions are entrusted to designated persons instead of involving the total membership in matters of governance.

Moreover, the ethos in communities changes from having a policy or rule for every aspect of communal life to relying upon a climate of trust and interpersonal rapport to guide covenantal living. As a community matures and members have a sufficient history together, procedures and rules are relaxed so a community depends more upon its tradition and *esprit de corps*.

This revising process does not occur because the order, in and of itself, is judged to be flawed. There are no perfect designs of order to be found. Revision results from the awareness that covenantal living is jeopardized by membership dissatisfaction with communal order. The present order may have served the community well, but the life transitions of members or the new personalities that have joined will cause a community to refashion its structures.

Communal life can be precarious. Communities are regularly dealing with financial crises that imperil their ministries. Koinonia and Patchwork Central have had to recover from fires that destroyed key facilities. The sudden deaths of Clarence Jordan at Koinonia and Lem Tucker at Voice of Calvary jolted these communities.

But membership dissatisfaction that leads to membership loss is the bane of communities. Maintaining the boundaries for a disgruntled or shrinking membership is disheartening. At best the maintenance causes fatigue; at worst it seems futile. Both results only exacerbate the dissatisfaction. Communal order goes through its most dramatic changes when members become distressed over their ability to sustain a committed and enthusiastic membership.

Rosabeth Moss Kanter's study of nineteenth-century communes stresses the importance of maintaining rigorous requirements for members. She concludes that the most "successful" (enduring) nineteenth-century communes enforced many commitment mechanisms. These mechanisms were rules, routines, doctrines, and procedures that ordered and defined group life. The greater the expectation for the individual to sacrifice, renounce, and invest, the greater the chance for communal success.[6]

Kanter's study provides significant insight into the power of such mechanisms to intensify individuals' commitment and group cohesion. Members' reluctance to change (or as often perceived by them, to dilute) the mechanisms of commitment is therefore understandable.

The five communities of this study, however, are testimony to the conclusion that thriving communities have learned how to adjust structures that impede communal purpose. The form of communalism must be adaptive to the function and temperament of group life. In other words, the value of structures must be assessed by their ability to deliver on communal expectations. Structures can be compromised; commitment will not.

Whether due to internal pressures associated with membership dissatisfaction or the external pressures of nonmembers' desires for inclusion, the alteration of structures will only be tolerated if members believe the integrity of the community can be preserved. The alteration may be a change in specific policies and practices. But at a more profound level it is the attempt to revive members' confidence in the ability of structures to fulfill the community's covenant.[7]

The disposition of members remains the key to communal vitality. And structures, whether old or revised, must satisfy *members'* understanding of intimacy and mission. To paraphrase Jesus' comments on the Sabbath, structures are made for members, not members for structures. Therefore, our most penetrating insights about structures result from studying them—not as perfected blueprints but as mechanisms that implement an evolving understanding of the holy order that serves the call to community.

For the Church Today

Most churches understand that their organizational structures are determined by denominational polity or administrative tradition. Members presuppose that decision-making practices are mandated by the principles and wisdom of the church's heritage. Matters of authority, membership criteria, and structures of commitment are addressed by a church's history. Unlike most intentional religious communities, congregations have deep roots in denominations that define procedures of organization. This rootedness nourishes the organizational life of congregations. Procedures are the result of many years of practice and debate. Authority and decision making are designated to clergy, laity, and committees in ways that honor theological and ecclesiological convictions. Corporate memory has a past full of stories that reveal how discipleship has been sustained by church order.

This rootedness can also lead congregations to be inattentive to pressing organizational needs. Members assume that tradition and polity sufficiently address the ordering of congregational life for discipleship. They may fail to assess how current practices empower members to fulfill their sense of call. Churches believe that old wineskins are adequate for the new wine entrusted to their keeping. Church structures must be continually evaluated to determine if they are capable of empowering the new spirit of commitment which flourishes.

By what authority is decision making guided in your church? Avery Dulles describes authority in the institutional church in which, "The Church is not conceived as a democratic or representative society, but as one in which the fullness of power is concentrated in the hands of a ruling class that perpetuates itself by cooption."[8] Or does authority reside with each member of your congregation?

Whether authority resides with a "ruling class" or the entire congregation, a major concern is the trustworthiness of that authority. Authority is not only the right to exercise power. It is also the ability to be trusted. Radical discipleship requires a religious fellowship where the governing authority that shapes intimacy and mission can be trusted.

In covenantal relationship, authority's participation in God's call is more important than its specialized knowledge. Submission occurs within a context of companionship in the spiritual journey. Experts about issues of intimacy and mission may stimulate our thinking and inform our commitment, but their insights will not motivate us to submit our commitment to them. Submission occurs out of trust that develops from a common commitment to follow God's calling. Persons with authority receive their integrity from being companions who know and love those who submit to their leadership.

Local congregations' dependence on authority has this requirement. When a church follows the organization dictated by its polity, the leaders and structures of authority retain credibility to the extent that they show themselves trustworthy. Covenant precedes submission. Consequently, it is crucial for a congregation to clarify its operative sense of covenant in addressing matters of authority and submission.

Authority is therefore not a permanent status defined by training or office. All members of a congregation are responsible to determine what is to be entrusted to decision makers and to assess their performance as authorities. If this trust is violated, then authoritative status can be withdrawn. Members confer authority. They challenge it. They authorize. They can give and withdraw their support depending on the trustworthiness of authority figures.

In this way, all members have opportunity to participate in determining the authority that rules the order of their congregation. Submission in covenantal relationship is a profound act of defining and acknowledging trustworthy authority.

How is authority determined in your congregation? Are some members excluded from positions of authority because of age, gender, theological beliefs, financial contributions, or length of time in the fellowship? How is authority demonstrated and proven trustworthy? Where in the church's life are members tutored in becoming authorities for the fellowship? How is submission practiced in your fellowship? Does your church order affirm the possibility of God speaking to your fellowship through every member?

Who are considered the authorities for matters of intimacy and mission in your congregation? Why are these persons or committees valued as trustworthy sources of guidance? How are their insights for directing the congregation's life tested?

Authority and submission are significant concerns of an intentional ministry. This is because they are the means by which calling and covenantal living are implemented.

How does your church *maintain the boundaries of community?* What criteria of membership distinguish those who belong to your fellowship?

Congregations will rely upon their denominational identity to define the meaning of membership. But understandings of denominational identity change from congregation to congregation and from individual to individual. If you were to ask members what it meant to be a member of their tradition (Presbyterian, Baptist, Mennonite, Methodist, Catholic, etc.), you would receive a broad range of answers.

Despite denominational affiliation, churches select which denominational policies and resolutions they will enact. Denominational affiliation does not necessarily translate into understanding the ethos and commitment of a local church.

Local congregations are also made up of members who have belonged to other church traditions before joining their present one. So while a Presbyterian church speaks of itself as conducting its life within the Presbyterian tradition, its members may be principally informed by their Baptist, Methodist, and Episcopal backgrounds.

I continually hear the lament of pastors who are frustrated by the multiple theological and polity orientations that compete with their church's denominational tradition in times of decision making. Denominational affiliation is no guarantor of clarity about a congregation's calling, covenant, or order.

Church membership is itself no guarantor of commitment to a congregation. Ask persons about the number of members in their congregation and the response is, "Do you want the official count of the membership roll or those who actually participate in the church?"

When I asked a Baptist official about the number of Baptists in the state of Georgia, he facetiously replied, "We have more Baptists than there are people living in this state."

The membership numbers of most churches have little integrity. Members are retained on church rolls long after they have terminated all association with a congregation (sometimes even after they have died).

But more disturbing is the realization that active members will minimize whether their belonging to a particular congregation discloses their commitment and discipleship identity. Beyond the rituals of joining, attendance at worship, financial contributions, and not being accused of immoral behavior, most members would be hard pressed to identify criteria of belonging. Members might attest to the importance of intimacy and mission to Christian witness, but it would probably be difficult for them to identify disciplines of intimacy and mission required by their church.

How do the rituals of joining your congregation and the classes for candidate members reveal the meaning of belonging to your church? Are the expectations of membership published and regularly affirmed by the congregation? In the intentional communities studied, there is not the problem of dispelling members who fail to live by the disciplines of their community. Each member so clearly understands the meaning of covenantal fellowship that they voluntarily leave when their commitment to communal purposes dies.

Is it possible for individuals to sustain their membership in your congregation after they have forsaken the commitment to congregational covenant? If so, what does this suggest to you about the relationship of covenant and membership?

These last two questions are not meant to suggest that members who fall short on fulfilling covenantal ideals should be outcasts from the congregation. Christian churches have been rightly criticized for shooting their wounded. The questions attempt to establish an awareness of whether the boundaries of community, as maintained by membership criteria, define the meaning of discipleship in your congregation.

Churches sometimes fear that being too specific and demanding about discipleship will discourage people from joining and participating. Recognizing the multiple responsibilities that compete for people's time, these churches will seek to assure persons that the church will not interfere with other obligations.

Perhaps this underestimates the people's hunger to participate in a religious fellowship worthy of the commitment demanded by faith. A transforming gospel makes demands that disturb our schedules and priorities. People who sense God's call know this. Spending less time outside the church is not the issue. The meaning of belonging to a fellowship is. Belonging can mean that members are devoted to work in contexts removed from the church. Yet the church remains a place of discernment and empowerment for their work. For example, a teacher of an inner city school overwhelmed by chronic poverty may be searching within her faith for the strength and hope to continue. Or a nurse may be desperately fighting to keep his heart sensitive to patients through the never ending days of sickness and death.

A strong membership identity can also help members determine how their involvements outside the church support or contradict the meaning of discipleship within the church. Church membership identity should inform how one functions in other contexts. Since the content of membership does not automatically come with denominational affiliation or being on a church roll, it is vital that a church continually reaffirm the meaning of belonging so belonging has meaning.

Reaffirming the meaning of membership will require congregations to evaluate their structures of commitment, decision making, and authority. The openness to assess and revise old structures, and the willingness to create new ones, will enable a congregation to make nurture of disciples a greater priority than following traditional organization. *By trial and error* congregations can gauge the effectiveness of different forms of church order to inspire, encourage, and empower members' discipleship.

Revising church structure is not new to churches. The operative organizations and procedures of decision making are frequently different than what is mandated by a congregation's official polity. In small churches with only one or two families, family members will have discussions and make decisions about the direction of the church without necessarily informing the pastor or calling an official meeting. These decisions are sometimes made in a family's kitchen where people gather for the sole purpose of eating and fellowship—but the business of the church surfaces, so the family decides. Large churches even have informal networks of discussion and decision making that are quite different than official procedures.

A challenge for congregations is the establishment of alternate structures that are not just the result of traditional ways of bypassing official structure or means by which an "old guard" retains control over decision making. Congregations need *intentionally* altered structures conceived to fit the new realities of their membership, the intimacy concerns of the fellowship, and the church's mission to society.

Every congregation has its unique mix of personalities that does not always conform to official procedures or traditional structures of church life. A policy which works well for the church across town may not resonate with your congregation. A congregation must find ways for members to feel that the church's organization empowers them to answer God's personal and corporate call.

This suggests that church organization should be as intentional and flexible as the necessities of discipleship and the variance in personalities require it to be. Radical discipleship can withstand failure, but it cannot thrive locked within traditional procedures for tradition's sake. Whether placing new members in significant leadership positions, finding ways for members to conduct mission that does not need official approval, or extending Christian education programs beyond the traditional times and traditional teachers, a congregation needs to have an experimental spirit ready to test the capabilities of new wineskins for the new wine under its stewardship.

CHAPTER 5

Transforming and Being Transformed

Prophetic Neighboring

Members of the five religious communities were asked to choose which of four statements corresponded most closely with their beliefs about social transformation. None of the members responded that "Social change is no responsibility of the religious community, since if individuals are soundly converted social problems will take care of themselves."

Thirteen percent indicated that "Social change is a partial responsibility of religious communities, but secondary to the transformation of individuals."

Eighty-one percent believed that "Social change is of equal importance with individual transformation."

Six percent responded that "Social change is even more important than individual conversion, since social conditions greatly affect individuals."

Clearly the members affirm social transformation as essential to Christian discipleship. But in addition to this, the members believe they are called to mission both to and *within* a particular place.

Voice of Calvary asserts, "The three R's of community development." *Reconciliation* is not only an act between God and humanity, but also an imperative for the local church as "a force and forum . . . across all racial, cultural, social, and economic barriers." Redistribution requires Christians to offer their resources, "skills, technology, and educational resources in a way that empowers people to break out of the cycle of poverty and become able to meet their own needs." But relocation is considered the first "r." The explanation given by VOC represents the conviction of the other four communities.

> In order to minister effectively to the poor, Christians need to relocate in the community [neighborhood] of need as part of a local body of believers. By living as neighbors with the poor, the needs of the neighborhood become one's own needs. Shared needs and friendships become a bridge for communicating the good news of Jesus Christ and working together for better conditions in the community.[1]

As discussed in chapter three, love is most effective when persons have access and proximity to one another. Social transformation is principally accomplished by being a caring neighbor rather than a commuting missionary.[2]

Communities employ a variety of methods to accomplish their goals of social transformation. The commitment to improve neighborhood conditions will involve communities in social service activities, neighborhood development, and neighborhood organizing as communal involvements that answer God's summons to faithfulness in a particular place.

Their record of accomplishment is extraordinary. Below are just *some* of the prophetic works of these communities.

Koinonia

Through such businesses as farming, processing and selling farm products, and constructing and rehabilitating houses, Koinonia has provided employment and income to neighbors (who are mostly black). When the seasonal demand for Koinonia products is high, up to sixty additional workers are hired.

Since 1969 the community has built over 180 houses for the poor in the county, with no-interest loans and no profit to

Koinonia. Koinonia has also repaired and renovated many of the earlier homes built.

Koinonia's Child Development Center (nursery and preschool) is a service to parents and children. Emphasizing motor skills, academic preparation for elementary education, nonviolence, cooperation, and issues of personal identity, the Center provides quality child care for up to forty-five children. A summer youth program of arts and crafts, recreation, and Bible study is sponsored for over fifty neighborhood youth.

Koinonia's members provide foster care to children, paralegal advocacy, home ownership counseling, and prison ministry (advocacy on jail conditions, legal representation of prisoners, visiting death row inmates). They are involved in the neighborhood outreach work of local churches, the National Association for the Advancement of Colored Peoples, and the Parent Teachers Association.

Sojourners

After moving to Washington, D.C., Sojourners became committed to addressing the housing problems of its neighborhood. Sojourners joined the Columbia Heights Community Ownership Project to halt real estate speculation, begin the process of buying buildings for low-income residents, and empower tenants to control their housing matters.

Members worked to develop a land trust that would give local residents influence in future neighborhood land development. They also organized tenants to combat exorbitant rent increases, the neglect of property in disrepair, and unlawful evictions. Sojourners' members were arrested when they sought to prevent evictions.

Eventually work with these various housing initiatives ended. Organizational conflicts and relentless power plays by landlords and real estate speculators stifled the effectiveness of such neighborhood organizing.

Sojourners organized recreational and discussion programs for neighborhood youth as well as a daycare ministry for about twenty-five children. A food club was established to enable neighborhood residents to buy food items at reduced commodity costs. Over 200 persons joined the club. Sojourners also began distributing free food commodities to neighbors on a weekly basis.

In 1983, the Sojourners Neighborhood Center opened. This large building became the locus for a variety of social change activities. The 1989-90 Annual Report indicated that sixty children (ages five-fourteen) registered for such programs as a weekly club (trips, art and language projects, presentations to the group), computer-assisted learning to help children with critical thinking skills, a teen group that focused on career development and health education, and other educational concerns. About fifty children registered for a seven-week summer program that offered recreation, art, crafts, reading development, a summer camp experience, and field trips.

Some twenty-six adults received individualized computer training to help them gain marketable computer and business skills. And the food distribution center served over 700 families and made 120 deliveries to homebound residents each month; in addition, over 500 people were enrolled in its program for distributing commodity supplemental food.

Church of the Messiah
Concern for neighborhood children caused Messiah to establish several mission programs. In 1973, the Messiah Learning Center was established as an alternative educational opportunity for neighborhood families. This resulted from Messiah assessing the quality of local public schools as unacceptable and beyond immediate reform.

Since Messiah's Common Life members who taught at the Center depended on the religious community for their economic needs, the Center had low expenditures for teachers' salaries. It therefore charged only $40/month for a child to attend. The Center eventually had about thirty students in grades one–six. During the summers, the church organized a summer youth program that involved recreational activities, arts, crafts, and Bible study. At times the summer program attracted over fifty youth (ages six–sixteen). A daycare center for children was started in 1976. Of the thirty-seven children enrolled in the program, thirty-two were from the neighborhood and did not belong to the church.

Messiah has had a long tradition of ministry to the mentally retarded, mentally ill, aged, and alcoholic of its neighborhood. With over 200 group homes in the neighborhood for the aged and mentally disabled, Messiah's ministry took neighborhood realities seriously. Sunday school classes, worship services, church programs, and visits to the group homes were approaches used to have a personal relationship with these persons and to involve their institutionalized neighbors in the life of Messiah.

Desiring to meet some of the economic needs of their neighbors, Messiah organized an exchange shop for clothing and a commissary to provide inexpensive food and household goods. Messiah also worked with local leaders to form a neighborhood organization that would address economic and social welfare issues (such as crime prevention). And when their neighborhood had an influx of immigrants (especially from Southeast Asia), Messiah organized its membership to assist them with transportation, education, and employment needs.

A major accomplishment of Messiah has been its renovation and management of neighborhood housing. The church began with a twenty-four unit apartment building, then purchased five duplexes. By 1990 (four years after termination of its Common Life arrangement), Messiah had repaired over 500 homes throughout Detroit neighborhoods, with about 200 in Messiah's immediate neighborhood. This is a significant record of improving the neighborhood by providing low-cost or free repairs for homeowners, and by increasing the availability of decent rental property for low-income residents.

Voice of Calvary
The letterhead of VOCM carries the organization's motto: "Pioneering in Black Christian Community Development Through the Church." As stated, when the word "community" is used at VOC, it refers to neighborhoods rather than an intentional religious fellowship. VOC is dedicated to reviving black communities by bringing church resources and Christian conviction to bear on their needs.

People's Development, Incorporated (PDI) was created to provide housing to low-income neighbors by purchasing, renovating, and repairing deteriorating properties. PDI financing facilitates the purchasing of some homes with low interest loans. Other residents begin as renters with the option to buy. PDI makes home ownership available to renters after they have demonstrated commitment to property stewardship through involvement in neighborhood meetings, attending PDI seminars, maintaining their homes and yards, increasing their formal education, receiving employment promotions, or becoming more financially stable. Since its founding, PDI has renovated seventy houses and plans to continue to provide renovated housing at a rate of eight-ten housing units per year.

The John M. Perkins International Study Center offers internships and seminars that address issues of community development, social justice, interracial relationships, and the Christian basis for involvement with these issues. Interns may stay one to two weeks, or those who want an in-depth experience may work at VOC for a year. Hundreds of interns have come to VOC to understand how their Christian commitment could be deepened by working for an impoverished black community. The interns have also been an important volunteer labor source for the various VOC ministries.

The VOC Family Health Center provides health care to low-income families, many of whom are refused as patients by other physicians. In addition to meeting immediate medical needs, the center is attentive to preventive health care concerns and the emotional stresses that effect the families' well-being. The small health care staff has had as many as 12,000 patient visits in one year.

The Thriftco Consumer Cooperative Center is part of the economic development objectives of VOC. The center offers low cost household items to its members. But VOC's purpose for establishing the center goes beyond providing inexpensive clothing and household goods. Thriftco is also intended to "provide jobs and training, to help the community to shape its social, political, and economic destinies, to create an avenue for evangelism, and to give the poor an opportunity to have ownership in an enterprise."[3]

Harambee Youth Ministries has offered a wide range of programs for local black youth. These include Good News Clubs (weekly Bible classes for children), tutoring services, a computer learning center, an after-school program of recreation and academic support, and volunteer assistance to the needs of a local elementary school. These programs have responded to the religious, educational, and social development needs of youth in their community. Most important, they have sought to enhance the self-image of youth who often feel hopeless about their chances to emerge from poverty.

Patchwork Central

From its beginnings, Patchwork members were responsive when its neighborhood experienced conflict. Whether racial tension at a public swimming pool or the threat of a local school being closed, the members have sought a just resolution to problems.

Their strategies for transforming their neighborhood are diverse. Often they have joined established neighborhood groups to protest governmental response to neighborhood issues. But Patchwork members have also served as decision makers in such influential organizations as the Evansville-Vanderburgh County School Board (the Patchwork member also served as president of the board); the board of directors for the InnerCity Cultural Center; the Evansville Urban Nutrition Coalition; the board of the Arts Council of Southwestern Indiana; and the Citizen's Advisory Council for Community Development Funds. Patchwork has also received grants to investigate, monitor, and assess community development projects to determine if federal monies were benefiting the low-income residents of Evansville.

Patchwork has generated programs that respond to ongoing neighborhood needs. Since 1981 Patchwork has operated an after school and summer program of recreation, arts, self-esteem perspectives, and interpersonal skills for neighborhood children. Hundreds of children have experienced these innovative programs, in which staff nurture and encourage creativity. Patchwork operates a food pantry that in 1991 served over 8,270 individuals. Periodically Patchwork has also sponsored health clinics, a shelter for battered women, counseling, concerts and plays, and seminars focusing on neighborhood issues.

In 1990, the Washington Avenue Health Care Center was established because of Patchwork's extensive commitment of time and resources. The Center operates in Patchwork's building, offering health care screenings, counseling, education, and referrals. Treatment deals primarily with "acute episodic problems." Serving a low-income clientele (who are either medically underinsured or not insured), the center receives about eighty clients per week.

Economic development has been one of Patchwork's key concerns. In addition to offering services to their neighborhood, its economic ventures have created employment opportunities. They established and operated a bakery. Persons have been assisted in finding employment. And since 1983, the Patchwork sponsored Neighborhood Economic Development Center has helped to develop businesses for low-income neighborhoods through technical and financial support.

Patchwork has sponsored an internship program to secure personnel for their various ministries. This has been viewed as a leadership development program for the interns and a staff recruitment mechanism for Patchwork's multiple projects.

After Patchwork purchased and renovated an empty synagogue and its facilities (renamed "The Meetinghouse"), the building housed Patchwork sponsored programs, social agencies (a housing counseling agency that prevents foreclosures, and a program that builds and renovates homes for the poor), and neighborhood organizing meetings. The Meetinghouse functions as an important center where neighbors are served and gathered to work for the well-being of their area.

Among area residents, churches, social agencies, and local government, Patchwork Central is known to be a persistent advocate for the poor and the development of their neighborhood. This reputation is hard won and deserved.

Social transformation for these communities is not limited to their neighborhood turf. Sojourners and Voice of Calvary have the goal of renewing churches for mission. They conduct workshops, send members to speak before outside groups, and publish materials to raise people's consciousness about Christian commitment and social issues.

All of the communities, whether or not it is their stated goal, do inspire individuals and churches to be involved in social outreach ministries. The communities tell their stories through regular publications and mailings of their life and work. At times they have been flooded by inquiries and guests who have the urge to see their example of Christian discipleship.

Sojourners magazine has had as many as 50,000 subscribers (down to 30,000 in 1992). Although most of the readers are in the United States, *Sojourners* also has a substantial international readership. Its articles, offering a Christian perspective on militarism, social justice issues, the peace movement, and racial reconciliation, have aroused thousands of readers to involvement with issues in their neighborhoods and demonstrations for peace and justice. Some readers have even formed local groups that use the magazine as a text for nourishing their spiritual life and mission activities.

Members of the five communities have been involved in demonstrations and acts of civil disobedience against the build-up of nuclear weapons, U.S. support of the Contras in Nicaragua and the right-wing government in El Salvador, the death penalty, and cuts in government spending for social programs. Sojourners has mobilized hundreds of people from around the country in marches and acts of civil disobedience against the arms bazaar in Washington, D.C., where military weapons were displayed for countries to purchase.

These activities beyond religious communities' neighborhoods are their effort to make an impact in transforming the larger society. All the while, they are defining the link between national and international issues and issues in their neighborhoods.[4]

In the prophetic tradition, these communities live a message that challenges structures of oppression and injustice. They criticize social systems that perpetuate poverty, racism, and militarism. They draw a sharp contrast between social realities justified and sanctioned by benefactors of the status quo and God's vision of a social order where the poor are empowered, diverse racial and cultural groups live together in freedom and justice, and international peace prevails over the will to dominate. The Old Testament prophets' message was not only characterized by criticism, but also by deep compassion. Their heart embraced the people. Injustice and abuse of God's people was heart-wrenching. So while the prophetic message was full of anger and condemnation, the prophet's love of God and compassion for God's people were even more characteristic of the prophet's witness.

The histories of these communities reveal the meaning of prophetic compassion within their neighborhoods. First, compassion is more than inspiring social ideals and consciousness raising. Compassion is caring for others with an understanding of their need that emerges from knowing them. Research that gathers data on social realities is important; however, one only understands issues fully when ongoing relationships are sustained with the people who are directly effected by the issues. Consequently, living in a location where one has the opportunity to care for another by being a responsive neighbor is crucial. The neighborhood remains the primary context for these communities to exercise their prophetic calling.

Second, prophetic neighboring is required of everyone in a religious fellowship. If only a few of a religious fellowship interact with neighbors, the witness of the fellowship is diminished. A religious fellowship loses its *corporate* sense of prophetic presence when some of its members withdraw from relationship with neighbors. Avoiding neighbors is not a prophetic option.

Third, caring for neighbors whose conditions are caused by complex social, economic, and political forces requires one to develop skills (and to recruit individuals with skills) for addressing their needs. Job training, remedial instruction, grant writing, and housing development are among activities that require more than a sympathetic heart. They also require a cultivated mind that understands how to engage institutions, bureaucracies, personal needs, and mechanisms of social transformation.

Fourth, prophetic neighboring is hard work that requires persistent involvement and financial investment. The complexity of neighborhood realities required that caring persons make the time and fiscal sacrifices to tarry with needs. Oppressive systems are not transformed by token gestures of concern but do respond to steadfast involvement and relentless commitment.

Prophetic vision without strategies for implementing the vision can leave people frustrated and politically impotent. The above implications of prophetic care are essential to radical discipleship that seeks to implement the commandment, "Love thy neighbor."

By Many Means Necessary

Blueprints for mission do not exist. The social outreach accomplishments of others can be helpful but do not eliminate the need to discern how mission must be adjusted for the particular social realities and personalities of one's locale. Mission is always an adventure into uncharted territory. The adventure teaches and guides.

The five communities have had to create and revise mission endeavors as the relationships with neighbors disclosed possibilities for mission. Their strategies of transformation are diverse, so that they might be relevant to the diverse nature of the problems they face.

In listing mission activities, several outreach methods are evident. *Neighborhood development* has tackled the economic and housing needs of neighbors by establishing businesses that employ neighbors as well as by building, renovating, and managing houses.

Neighborhood organizing has cultivated the leadership skills of neighbors and mobilized them to influence the well-being and direction of their locale through effective advocacy on pivotal issues.

Social service has provided neighbors needed commodities, information, counseling, training, and caretaking (especially with children).

Protests (marches, picket lines, civil disobedience) have given people a way to make their conviction public. They have increased participants' understanding about the political dimensions of issues.

Consciousness raising through publications and speakers bureaus has inspired nonmembers to support the religious community in its work. This has encouraged people to engage similar issues in their own church and locale.

Some members of Koinonia, Sojourners, Patchwork, and Messiah have earned their income by working in secular or church-related social service agencies. Their commitment to these agencies has gone beyond simply using them as a source of finances, for the members' work has been an expression of the Christian commitment which informs their call to their religious community. Although not sponsored by the religious community, the work has been appreciated by members as a labor of care that is consistent with their community's transforming purpose.

This conviction that one's work is an extension of one's discipleship commitment is evident in Patchwork Central members, who described themselves as "worker-priests." Judi Jacobson is an ordained United Methodist minister who operates a painting contract business. She relies on her house painting to provide the income that enables her to give her ministerial skills to Patchwork without needing a salary from the community.

But the worker-priest model is also a way of exploring discipleship matters. Jacobson says,

> Being a worker like everybody else [in the neighborhood] has helped me understand what everybody else goes through. It prompts me to put my theology up against my real-life experience and see what holds true and what doesn't. A lot of theological notions are pushed by working and being in business. For example, the basis of business is self-interest. What does Christianity teach but self-sacrifice? To balance those two is pretty difficult, but until those two are brought together, Christianity just doesn't hold water.[5]

Work in "secular" contexts can be sacred. All work is a means to exercise faith and to support transforming mission.

Mission programs sponsored by the communities have often been determined by members' training and temperament.

Youth programs were started by members whose educational background and interests prepared them for working with children. A nurse established a health care program. Members with computer skills initiated computer literacy programs to equip neighbors with job skills.

This strategy was evident at Patchwork Central, where new programming was dependent on members' interests and skills. Each member's gifts were celebrated as a patch that, when combined with other members' gifts, made a whole quilt. The strategy of shaping mission around the experience and motivation of members, however, has operated to some degree in all the religious communities.

Selected methods of social transformation are also determined by the personality of members. They may prefer providing services to individuals rather than the confrontation politics of civil disobedience. Or particular methods may reflect members' acquaintance with a limited range of social change options. They may have participated in providing services to the poor without ever envisioning the possibility of organizing them.

Even though the means of change are related to the experience and temperament of members, mission efforts are not confined by strategies within members' comfort zones. These religious communities have engaged in outreach efforts that require members to develop new skills, rely upon on-the-job training, and engage in new and frightening protest activities. Members may initiate a ministry that draws upon familiar skills, but their commitment to people often pushes them beyond the familiar.

The urgency of issues dictates the means employed. If the utility company is going to cut off the gas of poor people who cannot pay their bills, then some form of immediate public demonstration will be the most effective response.

Assessing the neighborhood's need for housing has also involved communities in development technicalities for which members had neither experience nor enthusiasm. Mission makes demands for which members are not prepared. The call to radical discipleship involves not only cultivating gifts and acting within familiar experiences of challenge. Radical discipleship responds to pain and oppression by employing necessary means of change—even if the first transformation must be increasing the knowledge and courage of the disciple.

Religious communities also come to realize that their mission work requires financial support and personnel beyond the capabilities of their membership. The demands of mission cannot be met by even the most extraordinary efforts of members alone. Nonmembers therefore become crucial to the effectiveness of communities' programs of transformation.

A few nonmembers are interns who may spend between a week to two years in a community. Some of these interns are exploring their interest in joining a religious community; other interns are fulfilling, through the communities' mission, a personal commitment to social transformation. Most nonmembers are volunteers who work with various communal programs, or they are financial contributors who support a community's business enterprises and mission endeavors. The communities expend considerable time and money to publish materials that inform supporters of their work and needs.

By assigning them interns and volunteers, denominations have recognized these communities as valuable contexts for discipleship. Sojourners and Patchwork have had interns from Mennonite service organizations. Patchwork has also had volunteers from the United Methodist domestic missionary program. Voice of Calvary has had interns from a missionary program of the Church of the Brethren. The Episcopal Church has given considerable funding to the ministries of Messiah, and Patchwork has received funding from the United Methodist Church. Drawing on the people and resources of denominations, whether through their official church structures or by appealing to individuals within the denominations, has been an important means of support for the work of these communities.

While religious communities are particularly invested in nonmembers who empower them to effect transformation, they also seek partnership with churches and neighborhood organizations that, though they may not be committed to the destiny of the religious community, will collaborate on specific mission programs and campaigns. The religious communities come to realize that fulfilling their call to mission requires the involvement of persons who have no commitment to communal covenant but who share the commitment to a transformed society.

To Make All Things New

Considering the enormous amount of time, energy, emotion, and finances poured into these ministries, the obvious question is, what difference do they make? Are these intentional communities effective models of social change?

Several conclusions can be drawn regarding the communities' approach to social transformation. First, discipleship must recognize that the poor live a precarious existence, which requires attention to their basic needs of food, shelter, and clothing. Whether through Sojourners' food distribution center, Voice of Calvary's Thriftco Consumer Cooperative Center, the food pantries, clothing closets for neighbors, or housing ministries which all of the communities operate, considerable energy has gone to basic physical survival needs.

Second, nurturing relationships with neighborhood children is vital to any hope for the next generation of adults. All the communities operate youth programs that provide a safe place for youth to receive attention to their emotional, intellectual, spiritual, physical, and social needs. Through educational programs, field trips, personal counseling, recreational activities, career development, and moral instruction, these communities prepare neighborhood children for life's challenges.

Each community has wonderful testimonies about the hundreds of youth shaped and changed by its programs. One of the most dramatic examples is that 300 of the 700 students in the elementary school in Sojourners' neighborhood failed to advance to their next grade level. In contrast, of fifty children attending Sojourners' afterschool program, only one child failed to advance.

Third, the communities recognize that employment opportunities are crucial to meeting the survival needs of neighbors. Koinonia employs neighbors in its businesses. Although the other communities have not established community owned enterprises that employ large numbers of neighbors, they have hired neighbors when salaried positions have become available in their ministries.

The religious communities do not have the resources to meet the employment needs of their locale. They are advocates for government and business to create work opportunities in their neighborhoods, but they are unable to establish significant programs that address employment by themselves. However, their work to improve educational performance, offer job training, and provide afterschool programs for working parents contributes to present and future requisites of employment.

Fourth, the identity of these religious communities became clearer for neighbors, and the communities' outreach efforts were enhanced, when buildings were bought for ministries. Because Messiah began with a church edifice, this shift in understanding and influence was not as pronounced. But where communities began in neighborhoods without buildings devoted to mission, their mission was better understood, and neighbor support increased, after the creation of a gathering place.

Such buildings symbolize investment and rootage in a neighborhood. They are new space for establishing new relationships. These buildings become structures that call neighbors together and embrace them with repeated experiences of care. They are tents of meeting where estrangement gives way to friendship and hurt is relieved by love.

Fifth, a new social reality depends on developing the leadership skills of neighbors, members, interns, and volunteers. Individuals who understand the forces of change in their lives and the means by which to effect transformation are vigilant long-term fighters for justice.

Accomplishing this with neighbors remains one of the most difficult challenges of these communities. Neighbors must give so much of their time and energy to surviving that they often do not have much left for the tedious work of neighborhood organization or development. They have also seen groups promising to fight for improvements come and go. They are therefore wary of any group, including these religious communities, that attempts to raise their expectations and reinvolve them in the battles for social change. Still these communities reached a small number of neighbors who share the vision of a new social reality and who cultivate their transformation skills through the ministries of the communities.

Sixth, efforts to transform the social order result in the transformation of the religious community and its supporters. Persons do not just have their leadership skills enhanced (although this does occur). Rather, they are fundamentally changed. Through involvement in social transformation they become aware of the complexity of social realities and the possibilities for altering them. They discover their own strengths and weaknesses as never before. And they are thrust into rethinking the meaning of being called to the intimacy and mission of community.

In conversations with a young white couple leaving Messiah, I asked about the difference the communal experience had made in their lives. They indicated they joined Messiah because of their commitment to racial reconciliation. The husband said, "We thought that by living in this neighborhood there would be the opportunity to further racial harmony by smiling and waving at our black neighbors. But this can be a hostile place to live where many [black] people don't really seem to want us here."

They were disappointed but wiser. Racism and its consequences have not been perpetuated because people do not smile and wave enough. The causes of racism are a tangled knot of complicated social, political, economic, and religious forces. The couple now understood this and realized that not only were they unprepared for their neighborhood's harsh realities, but they needed another environment in which to reconsider the meaning of their Christian commitment.

This kind of insight occurs with communities' members, interns, and volunteers. Naive assumptions crumble under the press of experience. The poor and oppressed are no longer abstract subjects of religious rhetoric and curiosity but are known as friends and strangers who love, threaten, encourage, disappoint, embrace, and reject. Whether members stay or leave because of their increased understanding, they see more clearly the reality of mission and the reality of themselves.

In the communities, the overwhelming majority of the members identify themselves as coming from a middle-class background. The move to their community is perceived as lowering (for most to a low-income level) their socioeconomic status. Nearly all of the members have college degrees and many have completed graduate degree work.

Voice of Calvary and Messiah have fluctuated in their percentages of black members, but have come close to a 50/50 black/white ratio. Messiah did not have many black members in its intensive Common Life living and economic arrangement. Patchwork never had a black member as part of its intensive Covenant life, but has increased black participation through its board and by lessening the requirements of Covenant involvement. Koinonia has had one and Sojourners two black members—and their involvement was quite brief. The socioeconomic profile of the communities' membership is in stark contrast to that of its neighbors.

This inability to attract a substantial poor and black participation in covenantal living is one of the greatest disappointments to these communities. They all attest to the importance of racial reconciliation, and they desire intimate relationship with African-Americans and poor people. Voice of Calvary began with black leadership and has continued with a significant number of black members. But even VOC is dissatisfied that more black volunteers and church members have not responded to their invitation to mission.[6]

The reluctance to join in covenant relationship with these communities may be attributed to several differences between the commitments of communities and the aspirations of black people and the poor. The commitment to simplicity emphasizes downward mobility; many poor and black people pour their energy into becoming more upwardly mobile—upward mobility is their escape route from life on the edge of survival to experiencing the "American Dream" of prosperity.

Commitment to submit to the authority of a community runs counter to the efforts of black people and the poor to have more personal control over their lives. Their condition of deprivation and oppression is felt to be the result of others making decisions for them and also a legacy of slavery. This matter is especially complicated for Sojourners, Patchwork (under its Covenant member arrangement), and Koinonia because they only have white leadership. Black people strive to support black leadership as their authorities. This is not to suggest that simplicity and submission to communal authority are antithetical to black people and the poor. It is to recognize that starting at the opposite end of the socioeconomic ladder gives neighbors a very different view of the steps by which life becomes more fulfilling.

The reluctance of neighbors to join the living and economic arrangements of Koinonia, Sojourners, and Messiah is also surprising because for many neighbors joining would bring an improved standard of living. The community members have decent housing, food, clothing. Life in community may be frugal, but it has more security than many neighbors experience.

Neighbors do respect the integrity of these communities' witness. The neighbors realize that community members have not joined to further their economic aspirations. Yet neighbors struggle to survive and improve their condition by joining *with* communities in mission rather than *in* communities' other covenantal commitments.

Though they do not become members of communities, neighbors and supporters dramatically alter communal life. Outreach expands a community's sense of purpose beyond the confines of the religious fellowship. Interaction with nonmembers keeps the community from becoming withdrawn and isolated. Outreach creates a channel that enables fellowship between the community and the larger world. The channel functions as a way for a community's commitment to flow out to meet, serve, and empower others.

But this channel is also an inlet. Just as members change the living situation of those outside the community, nonmembers change life in community. Those who need the expertise of communal members also have vital contributions to make *to* communities. The poor and oppressed have embodied courage and hope even when conditions have not improved. They have a testimony of God's sustenance in times of trial that inspires and renews community members. Lessons of faith and experiences of love have come from those who are the subjects of communal mission.

The volunteers who assist a community also have a strong impact on community members. These nonmembers are not considered to be hired hands or mere instruments of labor. They are integral to the lives of members. Genuine relationships of caring develop. The relationship with both groups of nonmembers energizes the commitment of communities and thrusts them all the more into the larger world. Because of outreach, when members return to the intimacy of their fellowship they, and therefore the fellowship itself, are never the same.

For the Church Today

What is your church's vision of a transformed social order? This question assumes that a congregation has an image of future possibilities toward which its mission is directed. Such an image is essential for every church as well as for intentional communities. "Where there is no vision, the people perish" (Prov. 29:18, KJV). Without an image, there is no imagination; and without imagination, energies cannot be devoted to a purpose. The fulfillment of Christian calling requires a vision. What is your church's vision and how is it made manifest?

A vision clarification exercise that I have frequently used with congregations is to ask small groups of members to draw a picture of the neighborhood that surrounds their church. Then draw images which indicate how the church relates to the realities pictured. Large group discussion ensues about the meaning of the various pictures and their symbolism.

Next I ask the groups to draw a picture of the future they desire for their neighborhood and to image how their church is related to these realities.

This exercise has always proved revealing for members. For many it is the first time that they have created and discussed visible impressions of their church's environment and their role in that environment. Drawing the pictures provides a clarity that eludes rhetoric alone. From the pictures, a congregation can begin to create a vision statement that informs its mission.

An envisioning exercise can begin immediately, but familiarity with one's environment is necessary before plans for ministry are completed. Congregations must know their neighborhoods; they must learn how to exegete their context. "Exegesis" is the interpreting of texts. In the church, the term refers to our effort to interpret passages of Scripture. A Bible study group might spend weeks studying a single passage of Scripture. The group will use concordances and Bible dictionaries to determine the original meaning of words. The writings of biblical scholars might be read to understand the historical setting or how other ancient source material changes the meaning of the passage.

Bible study groups exegete with such a time consuming and disciplined approach because they recognize the significance and complexity of the sacred text. There are depths of meaning which are only discovered through careful examination.

A church's neighborhood is the living text which, to be understood, requires sensitive and persistent exegesis. Congregations sometimes assume that because they are located in a neighborhood, they know it well. This assumption arises from having a presence in the community that allows them to *see* signs of stability, development, or deterioration. But knowing a community primarily comes through *listening* to it. And listening occurs through relationships with its people.

Frequently, churches conduct surveys and use census data to attain statistics about their community. While they may be sincerely motivated to develop a community profile that informs their mission efforts, if this is their only approach to understanding the community, they will miss knowing the people. People are not known through answers to surveys nor through computer printouts. The community's people are known best through relationship with them. It is in relationship that churches come to hear people's stories of their lives in the community—to hear about times of celebration and times of disappointment—to hear about fears and dreams that will only be told in a relationship of trust.

In her book *The Death and Life of Great American Cities*, Jane Jacobs describes the impact of city planners, developers, and architects on major cities in the United States. She presents cases where these professionals, in their efforts to improve city life, undermine the vitality of a community because they have not really understood the people and patterns of life in an area. These professionals plan according to their own notions of what a community needs. They will redirect traffic flow, or tear down distinctive architecture, or relocate old businesses that are gathering places, or move housing away from business districts. Consequently, in the name of progress they end up destroying anchors of identity and vitality for a community.[7]

The church in the name of mission can also have a destructive effect on its community when it assumes it can serve the community without knowing the community. When the implicit message of our mission strategy is, "We know what's good for you," the church's outreach is both arrogant and patronizing.

Howard Thurman warns of the danger of putting care before understanding when he writes,

> Intrinsic interest must be informed, and constantly. There is no substitute for hard understanding of more and more and more of another's fact. This serves as a corrective against doing violence to those for whom we have a sense of caring because of great gaps in our knowledge of their fact. This is generally the weakness in so much lateral good will in the world. It is uninformed, ignorant, sincere good will. . . . I think that this is why it is impossible to have intrinsic interest in people with whom we are out of living or vicarious contact.[8]

A congregation might assess its relationship with its neighbors by asking itself several questions. What are the names and stories of our neighbors? Or another way to ask this question: If residents in the church's locale were asked the question posed to Jesus "Who is your neighbor?" would the local church be identified? Have we had the kind of caring relationship with our neighbors so they know who we are? Or so they *experience* us as neighbors? Do they know our names and commitment?

So much local church mission begins with the effort to educate church members about conditions and issues. A church will conduct Bible studies on caring, sponsor panel discussions and watch films about the issues, and press members to examine the prejudices and fears that inhibit mission. All this is an effort to stimulate involvement by satisfying members' intellectual reservations. The operative assumption is this: if the mind agrees, the body will follow.

This approach can be effective for persons who are aroused principally by reason. But most of us resist involvement with our neighbors because of anxieties that rule our mind and emotions—anxieties that dominate because we fear what we do not know. In fact, the more we talk and strategize about being related to neighbors, the more they will loom as alien species that require Bible study and a panel of experts if we are to introduce ourselves and establish relationship. Such a method of preparation can reinforce the very fears a church hopes to eliminate.

Involvement with neighbors, for many of us, would best occur if we were seized by experiences of relating to neighbors. Sometimes we must be led to places for which we do not feel prepared by our knowledge—places where we feel that the experience of relationship is thrust upon us. Such encounters come through attending community meetings, parent-teachers association meetings (even when church members may not have children in the local school), and other events where neighbors gather. Encounters also come through conversing with neighborhood youth playing on a church's basketball court or in a local park or talking with senior citizens at their center; through volunteering to assist social service agencies in their work with neighbors; and through relying on neighborhood leaders to introduce us to neighborhood people. Sometimes we must trust that if the body goes forward, the mind and heart will follow.

Prophetic neighboring occurs from caring relationship. A congregation need not wait for a crisis or catastrophe to happen before it relates with neighbors. To wait would suggest that neighboring is only a response to someone's problems or weakness. A caring neighbor seeks to be in relationship because the relationship itself is valued. Conversations occur that do not necessarily result in decision making or action. Rapport is established without the need to have a political agenda. This basis of neighboring emphasizes a fuller range of emotions with another—joy and pain, boredom and excitement, expectation and despair, frustration and achievement. Neighboring only in crisis suggests that one is solely responsive to another's inabilities. Being a constant neighbor provides more opportunities to experience and appreciate the whole person. A neighbor who has tarried with the heart of another during normal times is more likely to know how to care during crisis.

Caring for another also means determining the root causes which threaten another's well-being. Neighbors have problems not addressed with a smile and a wave. Christian disciples need skills of analysis and action that enable them to wrestle, *by many means*, with the complex social structures and forces that affect neighbors' lives.

Certainly congregations should begin by discerning their immediate abilities to do mission. Too many churches have never taken an inventory of the wealth of knowledge and skill resources which are resident within their membership. But caring should never be imprisoned by present abilities. Other people's needs can stretch our imagination and our willingness to become capable of enacting our imagination.

Individuals and congregations will not only need to expand their skills and abilities. They will also need to work cooperatively with other churches and civic organizations to bring about needed change. A committed church will frequently fail to influence social realities because it only considers what *it* can do about issues. No contact is made with other neighborhood churches. Civic organizations are not perceived as mission partners. Even soliciting support from among the churches of one's own denomination is never pursued.

Why? In part, many of our churches have a Lone Ranger tradition of ministry. They have always done it by themselves. Perhaps they believe it is simpler to plan and execute without the myriad problems that result from working with other groups. Or perhaps they take more pride in projects that do not require them to share the credit with others.

Whatever the reasons for our individualism, our neighbors

have concerns for which cooperative mission is a necessary means of transformation. When it asks the question "Who are our neighbors?" a congregation should envision (along with individuals and families) other religious fellowships, civic organizations, businesses, and social agencies. Cooperation can empower congregations to have more resources for a single strategy of ministry. Cooperation can also relieve congregations from trying to do everything when multiple facets of an issue require attention. As with the experience of religious communities, networking with nonmembers and organizations becomes a necessary means.

Jules Henry's *Culture Against Man* is a scathing critique of modern forces working to replace values of support and nurture with values of domination and exploitation. After examining societal policies and systems, Henry perceives a well-orchestrated effort that threatens humanity.

> Where is the culture of life? The culture of life resides in all those people who, inarticulate, frightened, and confused, are wondering "where it will all end." Thus the forces of death are confident and organized while the forces of life—the people who long for peace—are, for the most part, scattered, inarticulate, and wooly-minded, overwhelmed by their own impotence. Death struts about the house while Life cowers in the corner.[9]

Henry not only describes our condition but also provides a prescription. If we are to challenge the structures that threaten the vitality of our society, and if we are to do more than feel good about doing more, then becoming organized with others who desire a nurturing and affirming social order is essential.

Our congregations need to become vigilant participants in organized efforts to influence social realities. Systems of oppression and injustice do not change because of do-gooders dabbling with issues. Even when an issue generates a public outcry and receives extensive publicity, policy makers expect to continue with business as usual when no ongoing interest group promises to maintain the pressure for change. Disciples of transformation must be tenacious. The integrity of discipleship and the effectiveness of any means of transformation depends on it.

Is God's call that the church be a transforming fellowship too demanding? Can the church really make a difference in the social order. Or is society beyond the church's influence? These questions are seldom asked by congregations. Yet the lack of prophetic involvement of many churches suggests clergy and laity do not harbor much hope that their churches can *make all things new*. They are cynical about their fellowship being God's instrument of social change.

It would be instructive to ask members of your church how they feel about this matter. Is your local church able to be God's fellowship of transformation? What prevents the church from relating with the social concerns of God's world? Has God given up on your congregation serving the people for whom God is concerned?

The faith task before congregations is not to contemplate social outreach by weighing the odds of converting all systems and individuals to an idealized image of the good society. We are called to care regardless of the odds for cure. We do not visit a hospital only if we can be sure the patient is becoming well; we visit because caring makes a difference. AIDS patients often say that their physical battle with their deadly disease is not as traumatic as their experience of abandonment. Love is not dependent upon conditions. Whether conditions are destructive or nurturing, love persists and prevails.

This is good news! When caring bonds lives together, conditions may remain the same but all things are new! The steadfast companionship of caring persons redefines reality.

Sojourners is located in a high-crime section of Washington, D.C., where the tragedy described in the following statement from the Centers for Disease Control occurs regularly: "It is now more likely for a black male [in Washington, D.C.] between his fifteenth and twenty-fourth birthdays to die from homicide than it was for a U.S. soldier to be killed on a tour of duty in Vietnam."

Sojourners' neighborhood work has not altered this trend. And the other three urban religious communities cannot claim that their ministry has lessened problems with crime. But neither does the prevalence of crime cancel their witness of love. Because one loves deeply, all necessary means are taken to improve conditions. Debilitating conditions are not tolerated as unreal or inconsequential. Love feels pain and suffering and gives itself fully to tackling their causes. If the causes persist and conditions do not change, love continues to transform. Abandonment is transformed into fellowship, strangers become companions, life adrift receives guidance, relationships of affirmation occur in climates of negation, steps toward freedom are taken though all signs read "no exit," and despair gives way to hope.

These transformations are also experienced *within* congregations in mission. Members are surprised to receive blessings they assumed were theirs to give the "less fortunate." Church members are made new by their experiences of caring. Our churches' soup kitchens and night shelters serve the poor, our meeting rooms provide a space for neighborhood organizing and personal counseling, members volunteer to assist hospitals by holding infants and they assist hospices by embracing the dying. How easy it is to characterize this labor as "giving." In caring relationships, however, one is always giver and receiver, host and guest. Mission is always the petition for the privilege of entering another's heart. When granted, we must take off our shoes, for we are then standing on holy ground.

Radical discipleship is forged in mission. As the subjects of mission become real, the meaning of faith, hope, and love become increasingly clear. In mission, the call to community is answered and reinterpreted and answered and reinterpreted, by trial and error and trial again. Our success in transforming conditions is never assured. But we (members and neighbors) will definitely be changed. And the empowering presence of God is experienced as never before.

CHAPTER 6

To Know the Promise of Promise

Respecting Common Miracles

The call to community is experienced as a promise. The hearers sense they are invited into a fellowship most able to fulfill their desire to be faithful to God. Although the future remains uncertain, the conviction that they are called by God to this context of discipleship is reassuring. When God calls people, God sustains them in answering the call. And when God sustains, life is blessed.

The critical question is this: Are intentional religious communities viable models for disciples to experience the promise of Christian commitment? The previous chapters have hopefully answered this question with a resounding "Yes!" Members of communities studied attest that living in covenant with others has deepened their faith and empowered their witness to God's world. Even persons who have left or not joined these communities declare that these communities have challenged and inspired them to a fuller Christian commitment. These communities have persevered as a prophetic force in their particular locations and beyond.

Though a "yes" is given, we have seen that intentional communities are rife with problems. The required high levels of commitment and sacrifice are not for everyone. The demands of communal maintenance can be exhausting. Membership and communal structures can be so fluid that a mood of instability can threaten life together. Members grow tired of always revisiting matters of conflict and re-envisioning structures of resolution. Perhaps most disturbing to the communities themselves, their communal covenants and structures are so alien to neighbors' experience that the communities fail to attract neighbors as members.

Intentional communities are not perfected fellowships for discipleship. But the value of a witness in our midst should not depend on its perfection. Perfected models of discipleship do not exist. If we are trapped by the need to discover the perfected or near perfect model (whatever that means), then we will be disappointed with all living examples. Someone we love dearly and who brings joy to our days is *not* many desirable things. But to define persons by what they are *not*, rather than by what they *are*, distorts their significance. The same is true for assessing intentional communities. These communities are *not* many things that we might want in a religious fellowship. But what they *are* is both nurturing and inspiring for discipleship.

Intentional communities have glorious periods when membership increases, internal harmony and cooperation prevail, programs flourish, and support is abundant. They also have distressing times of membership loss, communal discord and conflict, jeopardized outreach, and a waning of support. If their difficulties cancel the value of their contributions, then all discipleship is in vain. God's promise to be our God and that we will be God's people, offers no exemption from travail. God's promise does not avoid but survives trauma. Crises, frustration, and failure are elemental realities of discipleship. We are assured, however, that God will abide with us. And with this assurance we are emboldened to be disciples.

Intentional communities remind us that commitment always requires sacrifice. They challenge our choices of affluence and materialism. They expand our understanding of identification with the poor and oppressed. They redefine stewardship and servanthood beyond notions of tithing and volunteerism. They stress the necessity of intimate relationship with those who join together in Christian fellowship. All the while they make obedience to God the primary basis for decisions.

The value of intentional communities as models for the church is belittled by critics who focus on the tendency of such communities to be short-lived. Longevity becomes the decisive criterion for determining their worthiness as models. Although the five communities of this study have remained viable fellowships despite crises and dramatic changes in their structure, their existence also remains precarious. Like many storefront churches (those small urban churches seen in facilities previously used by a business), most intentional communities are organized and terminated within a relatively short period of time.

Sociologist Rosabeth Moss Kanter responds to the conclusion that longevity equals viability when she says,

> The failure rate of communes is high, but so is the failure rate of small businesses. And no one is suggesting that small business is not a viable organizational form. As the commune movement grows, so do the number of groups that build for themselves what it takes to succeed as a commune.[1]

This small business analogy is helpful for putting their terminations in perspective. More relevant is the centrality of the cross as a Christian symbol of commitment. If success is a category of Christian discipleship, it has to do with obedience rather than escaping death. Three years of obedient service that results in death is better than three hundred years of maintaining life by avoiding perilous commitments.

Martin Luther King, Jr.'s, statement, "If a man hasn't found something he is willing to die for, he isn't fit to live," also applies to religious bodies. For what purpose would your church be willing to die? Jesus accepted the cross as the consequence of his commitment; are disciples greater than their master? Is faithfulness unto death no longer required? These questions are not advocating that Christians acquire martyr complexes. Neither are the questions naively assuming that death is always the logic of commitment. Some churches die because their spiritual life stagnated. The fundamental conviction being pursued in this questioning is whether physical survival is a higher priority than living one's commitment to God.

Institutional church leaders will dismiss the usefulness of intentional communities as models for the church because the communities do not completely mirror the dynamics and membership profiles of local congregations. To shut ourselves off from the life-giving power of another's story is a perspective for death. Our vitality and salvation depend on our ability to recognize God's activity in unexpected places and to be guided by it.

How easy it would be to ask how an individual who lived 2000 years ago—in a culture so different from our own, poor and oppressed, rejected by the authorities of the religion to which he was devoted, and executed as a criminal—could serve as the model of faith for billions of people throughout the ages. Yet Christians declare that their hope is based on nothing less than following this person from Nazareth as Lord and Savior.

God is continually providing us witnesses whose commitment and work reveal God's heart. They perform miracles, and perhaps as important (considering their ability to bring vitality to that which was dying), they themselves are miracles. Because we know their limitations, and because they are familiar to us, we easily overlook their significance.

They are not *respected* for what they are and do. But respect must be given if we are to know the fuller meaning of God's promise. *Respect* literally means (spect) to "watch," "see," or "observe," (re) "again." To "look back on" or "to see again" is basic to appreciating the true value of someone or something. Conclusions drawn from cursory glances will not suffice. We must tarry with others if we are to begin to know the presence of the holy.

Intentional communities are miracle-working miracles that transform individuals, society, and the church. In respecting them, God's promise becomes evident. We see how a committed people willing to live sacrificially for God are able to care for one another and for society in ways that amaze and astound. With few members and limited economic resources, they establish creative fellowships that enable persons to experience God's promise.

The experience is personal; people gain a new sense of self

that provides a greater awareness of their identity and worth as God's children. The experience is relational; the sanctity of knowing and being known by another tutors and comforts the heart. The experience is social; neighbors and strangers become known as persons (not just conditions) to whom we are bound.

The miraculous impact of communities goes beyond their corporate witness. As stated, they inspire persons who neither join them nor join in their various ministries, but who are emboldened to serve God because of them. In addition, the five communities studied have given birth to significant independent organizations of transformation.

For example, Millard Fuller, the founder and Executive Director of Habitat for Humanity, started Habitat because of his involvement with Koinonia Partners. Habitat has built over 15,000 houses in thirty-six countries (approximately 800 cities). Jubilee Partners began as a community formed from Koinonia members. Since 1979 it has resettled refugees fleeing persecution in Central America, assisted war victims in Nicaragua, and cared for death row inmates in Georgia. Voice of Calvary has assisted in the establishment of health centers which have cared for thousands of persons in rural Mississippi. Church of the Messiah's work created a major housing renovation corporation in Detroit. Communities give birth to organizations that become vital witnesses to God's love and power.

Congregations are also miracle-working miracles. Churches and their members offer extraordinary care. Congregations support schools, finance missionary work, and lobby for life-giving welfare legislation. They rally to undergird individuals and families in crisis. They sponsor counseling centers and a wide array of therapeutic services. Individual members care for foster children, give themselves to persons through their vocations, and provide comfort to the grieving. Their discipleship is neither publicized nor touted. In a quiet manner, they serve.

Congregations have marvelous corporate and individual expressions of steadfast love that transforms conditions and hearts. As with intentional communities, familiarity with congregational life, and the desire for even greater influence, can leave a congregation's members unimpressed with its present witness. Although transforming power abides, members do not draw from it as a source for renewal. Familiar work must be respected if its miraculous character is to be celebrated and available as a resource for encouraging the discipleship of a congregation.

The invitation to see the word made flesh is the invitation to perceive God's movement thriving in our midst. Unimpeded triumph this is not! God's movement can be seen in the transitory, the defeated, the countercultural, and the familiar. Intentional communities and congregations perform miracles of intimacy and mission that assure us of God's promise to claim and empower us. While radical discipleship is sustained by its commitment to the future which the God movement brings forth, it is also sustained by respecting the signs of what God is already doing.

Risking Modest Proposals

How amazed we are when Christians do what they profess. Whenever a church feeds the hungry, serves the poor, cares for the sick, attends to the needs of prisoners, and conducts ministries of justice and reconciliation, we are awed by such bold and faithful discipleship. After hearing so many *reasonable* explanations for churches' inability to be in mission, we grow accustomed to timid churches. So when a church embodies the gospel's caring examples, we are inspired in ways that betray our great hunger to experience faith in action.

The gospel is radical. In spite of our contorted logic and theology that would make the gospel capitulate to our prejudices and fears, God is under no obligation to compromise. We are called to serve in a movement that transforms all relationships to reflect God's passion. Our response to this is either "yes" or "no." Our "yes" is felt as blessing; we know that fulfillment is dependent upon faithfulness to God. Our "yes" is also threatening; not only will others be transformed, but we will be transformed even when we prefer the *status quo*. Being faithful to a radical gospel is not easy, but this we must do.

Too often Christians present a vision of a radically new order without helping people to understand how one arrives there.

The vision is inspiring, yet paralyzing. While the vision has esthetic value for all Christians, it seems to only have practical value for super-Christians. Ironically, radical discipleship is instructed by modest proposals. The radically new results from initially modest endeavors on its behalf.

I have sometimes wondered if our rhetoric about a radically new social order was intentionally used to discourage Christians from doing anything. In consulting with congregations, I work with pastors and laity who decry their members' unwillingness to confront massive social ills. They rail against racism, the brutality of capitalism, the insensitivity of politicians, and the failure of social institutions. I am continually surprised, however, by their reticence to try the simplest efforts that relate to these ills.

If I suggest they introduce themselves to their neighbors about whom they feel so deeply, nervousness and futility pervade our discussion. Someone will insist that the problems are too systemic for individuals to effect. Another voice will indicate how extraordinary human and financial resources are needed *before* a group can influence conditions. The impossibility of receiving support from the *total* congregation is considered a barrier.

Those who see benefits from this exercise of introduction will quickly point out the many areas of need which are not resolved by it. The rhetoric of radical commitment disguises their fear of being involved with neighbors. Their radical vision has resulted in Christian inertia.

Christian discipleship is empowered by modest proposals. They help get Christians started. Rather than being faced immediately with a challenge for which persons are completely unprepared, modest proposals invite them to participate at their current level of readiness. The call to radical discipleship is the call to do what we have the power to do.[2] To do less is the sin of sloth, to expect more is the sin of arrogance. Both are sin! The integrity of proposals for ministry depends on their ability to incorporate this principle.

It might even motivate Christians to know that they are receiving a *modest* proposal. When a preacher or lay leader presents an opportunity that requires extraordinary courage or time, we easily admit our inability to qualify for the challenge. But to refuse to give our commitment, after hearing how the opportunity has been designed in consideration of our limitations, leads to embarrassment and appropriate guilt. Modest proposals invite persons to servanthood with a disarming viability.

Realizing our ability to engage issues with current resources is important to initiating discipleship. Church members will often gather around a social concern and conclude that they need to recruit a larger group *before* they begin to address the concern. Such groups remain disappointed with the numbers of people who respond to their appeals. They meet to discuss the need for a larger meeting rather than proceeding with those present. When others join them, the new recruits do not experience enthusiasm about the social concern; rather, they hear complaints about the absence of needed persons for the meeting. Whenever two or more gather to witness, they should focus on how their commitment can be exercised.

Encouraging others to join them is important. But others are more likely to be persuaded by seeing a few actually doing something to gain information or to be in relationship with neighbors than by a group delaying action until it can amass a critical number for ministry. When disciples focus on what they do not have, rather than on what they have the power to do, they tend to emphasize their impotence. They therefore miss taking advantage of opportunities that are only seen when immediate resources are valued.

This insight was illustrated for me when a community organizer met with a group of angry suburban homeowners. They were upset that the developer of their new subdivision was refusing to correct problems occurring on their properties. Although the developer still had an interest in the subdivision, because it had homes he wanted to sell, he would not agree to fix the problems. And since their homeowner's contract forbade posting any protest or political signs in yards, he did not worry that they would scare away new customers.

When the organizer asked about the rights they had, they resignedly said their only option was to sell their homes. The organizer then suggested that everyone put a "For Sale" sign in their yards. He reasoned that anyone looking to buy a new home in the area would be suspicious of all the signs indicating that current residents wanted to unload their properties. The homeowners did this. Soon the developer cooperated.

Modest proposals are also characterized by encouraging disciples to establish contact with *persons* and not just issues. Recruiting church members to overturn an oppressive economic system can feel overwhelming and impersonal. Asking members to establish a caring relationship with one poor family needing support to survive can involve members with individuals *and* the oppressive economic system. This enables members to know not only the statistics of poverty, but the expressions, scents, frustrations, resilience, wisdom, and complexity of the people who are poor. Relationships with the subjects of issues are crucial to informing our work with larger structural matters. Mission without intimacy jeopardizes the possibility of knowing the subjects of our concern as companions who tutor our mission and enrich our lives. Intimacy without mission severs a relationship from renewing transcendent sources of love.

This emphasis on modest proposals is not a retreat from the complexities of systemic change. To the contrary, modest proposals can be a means for introducing persons to systemic issues. Persons who will resist asking critical questions about capitalism or the government's role in social problems will begin to raise the same analytical questions as they attempt to understand and remedy the problems of families they know. Becoming involved at a personal level can inspire and empower disciples to deal with the policies that imperil the people they love. Modest proposals can lead to dramatic transformations.

In congregations where members wish the church was a more caring fellowship, modest proposals of intimacy could prove useful. For example, the membership might be organized so every member was responsible for maintaining a friendship with and praying for two other members. The membership could also be organized into small groups where persons have a place to disclose their heart and experience the love of others. A simple idea—initiating a process that would assure members that they are embraced in the heart of another. What difference might it make in our churches if every member felt the companionship of other church members? How might other possibilities for caring relationship be generated by such an interpersonal covenant?

Modest proposals for mission could provide an opportunity for every member to have a hands-on experience with a social concern. Members could be asked, as an act of discipleship, to commit themselves to at least one community organization or activity that attends to the needs of people. Every church could accept the challenge to sponsor at least one outreach ministry in their immediate neighborhood.

These mission commitments could be affirmed by a church agreeing to celebrate periodically the outreach of its membership. Through liturgy and storytelling, the congregation would bring before God the successes, failures, clarity, and doubts of its involvement with God's world. In worship we come to know, in ways quite needful to our spirit, the promise of God's covenant to be with us and God's renewing power.

We waste opportunities for service because we underrate our ability. The needs are enormous and our resources seem too few. Perhaps a difference can be made by persons with five talents, but since we have only one, burying it seems safer than putting it to work. Jesus tells us that such a strategy angers God for it does not honor God's expectations of us and God's way of empowering servants to serve (Matt. 25:14-30). A modest proposal functions like a talent. It is a resource entrusted to us—making it possible to fulfill God's desire.

Modest proposals are *risky* because, while the proposal itself is modest in relation to needs, the consequences can be severe. As persons are introduced to the conditions and pain of others, the world is redefined. People will become angry because of the reality they now see. Some will be hostile toward the church as the agent of seeing. When its members are disturbed, the church is disturbed. Modest proposals quake the very ground on which we have come to depend.

This is why modest proposals are met with great resistance. God is more intimately known, however, through the shaking of our foundations. Our reality, which seemed so securely structured, crumbles. Guarantees of durability prove worthless. The promises of God stand long after our best designed enterprises falter. God is known as our ultimate security and enduring reality. In risking modest proposals we come to know how radically secured we are.

Intentional communities are modest models. Their many covenantal and social change ministries are not assaults on the citadels of power. There are key social issues they cannot significantly influence. Much of the institutional church ignores their witness. Still intentional communities do what they have the power to do. And in doing this, they amaze us with miracles of care that inspire our vision of discipleship.

In 1957, Koinonia was met by a delegation of prominent white citizens from Americus, Georgia, who believed that the religious community should be terminated. The spokesman for the group said to Koinonia's members,

> Now your experiment has provoked the sensibilities of a vast majority of our people . . . We came out here on the basis that you are serving what you believe to be Christian principles . . . Now our philosophy is that the first duty of a Christian would be to . . . make brotherly love in the community. Unfortunately, your experiment has not done that. It has set brother against brother; it has created bitterness; it has created hatred; it has created every emotion that is contrary to my concept of Christianity. . . . It is our belief that unless this experiment is moved to other fields that tempers will get to such a point that somebody is going to be hurt. . . . We want to appeal to your good judgment to pray over it and think over it and see if you don't think you'll be serving the best interests of the community and certainly the best interests of your Lord to move and leave us in peace.[3]

Koinonia was bearing witness to a modest proposal that black and white people could work and eat and fellowship and worship together on a farm. This traumatized the white citizens of Americus and inspirited the religious and moral imagination of people, both nationally and internationally. The social order and religious faith were challenged and transformed by Koinonia's commitment to be a modest paradigm of a radical gospel. Such a commitment leads to radical consequences.

The call to radical discipleship is reassuring and disturbing. Anytime we are provided opportunities to bear witness to the beliefs that claim us, terror seizes. Stripped of excuses, we are called to account for our choices, and ultimately our lives. But choice we have. There is something we can do, no matter how modest, to express our commitment to being in covenant with God. If we give ourselves fully to God's call and opportunities, not only will others be amazed, but we will also be astounded by what God has accomplished through us and in us.

Embraced by the Heart of the Matter

Common miracles inspire us. Modest proposals provide a way to enact our commitment. Being embraced by the Heart of the matter grounds our discipleship in love—a love so deep that the word *affection* does not sufficiently depict how it drives our very being; closer to defining its impact is *passion*. Radical disciples are extreme lovers, obsessed with their loving relationship with God. God is their passion. And to be passionate about God is to be passionate about relationships of intimacy and mission.

> Those who say, "I love God," and hate their brothers or sisters, are liars; for those who do not love a brother or sister whom they have seen, cannot love God whom they have not seen. The commandment we have from him is this: those who love God must love their brothers and sisters also. (1 John 4:20-21, NRSV)

Passion is not just the means to intimacy and mission. But intimacy and mission are the means by which one's passion is fed. The fire that burns within us must be fueled by its environment—intimacy and mission keep our fire from suffocation and exhaustion.

A church will be forgiven for many deficiencies (a weak-voiced choir, poor preaching, boring liturgy, deteriorating buildings), but it will not be forgiven for indifference. Caring relationship is essential to its identity and its vitality. Passion for the vitality of others is required for a vital faith that calls people into a vital fellowship that seeks to obey the very Source of vitality. To repeat the song's refrain mentioned at the beginning of this study, "They will know we are Christians by our love, by our love, yes they'll know we are Christians by our love."

Love defines reality. The testimony of religious persons throughout the ages is that the universe has a Heart. Love authors and governs the physical laws and biological processes. Love is our hope for understanding reality and our calling within it. Radical disciples depend upon love to image reality and its meaning. Such imaging is always suggestive, for reality will not be fully captured by our descriptive efforts.

Artists know this. The poet's metaphors usher to a realm where words cannot go. The painter's color and form take the observer to places beyond the dimensions of canvas. The musician's rhythm and tone carry the listener, faster than the speed of sound, to heights and depths. Likewise, the disciple's caring reveals and guides to a deeper truth.

Our discipleship provides only partial disclosure because mystery is God's nature. We speak our devotion, but the experience of God is finally unspeakable. The wonder of God is beyond words, beyond all attempts to image. Rather than explanation, we are inspired to ecstasy and reverence. To explore God's mystery never results in knowing how deep God is, but only in some realization of how shallow God is not.

But explore and speak and image we must do because even our inadequate efforts reveal and sustain our passion to be embraced by God's heart. The challenge before intentional communities and congregations is to live their discovered truth, and always to search for truth. When communal and congregational intimacy are inhibited by cliques or the refusal to bear one another's burdens, and when mission cowers before the enormity of social need, Christian disciples are able to persevere when they are embraced by their passion.

Life seems too complex for such a simple conviction. Legion

are the theological tomes which have rightly concluded that discerning strategies of discipleship is often bewildering because of the complexity of the church and world. But complexity can be navigated when we are guided by the correct principles of discernment. Immense variables are seen to have an underlying unity that steadies and reveals.

By way of analogy, cosmologists seek to devise a grand unified theory that explains how the fundamental forces of the universe are governed by physical laws. Billions of dollars are spent on particle accelerators, super computers, and other expensive equipment to support the research that attempts to provide an equation that explains the dynamism of the universe. Technology for testing some preliminary assumptions does not yet exist, if it ever will. These cosmologists push scientific knowledge and technology to its limits in pursuit of their theory.

I was stunned to hear one of the leading cosmologists indicate how they would recognize this theory that might be unprovable by any physical means of testing. He said such a theory would distinguish itself from other competing theories by its "simplicity and beauty."

Love, as the discerning principle of discipleship, is also known for its simplicity and beauty. The most complex human arrangements succumb to it as the unifying principle of vitality. Laws, social policies, customs, governance, and stewardship are ultimately evaluated by their furtherance of love. Love brings relationships into harmony with the rhythm of God's heart.

Also there is a simplicity to love, such that persons who have no formal education and have never traveled beyond the boundaries of their village understand it as thoroughly—and often better—than scholars and globe-trotters. The storefront church may exhibit its meaning more clearly than the nearby cathedral. Centuries of interethnic hostility will crumble as reconciliation is trumpeted by a prophet with a simple dream. Disciples are amazed by the simplicity of their passion; so much so, that we often distrust its power.

Love is also beautiful. It inspires. Love ushers us into a realm of appreciation where the true value of life becomes evident. The sacredness of creation is known to us, and reverence characterizes our relationship. Individuals are not valued according to their virtues or vices. Persons are not defined by their condition. For love loves; in so doing, we come to experience the true identity and worth of persons as beloved ones of God.

Evelyn Underhill has said that "beauty is simply reality seen with the eyes of love."[4] Disciples caring for one another and the world will encounter ugly realities, but love transforms and beauty shines forth. Our passion has esthetic appeal that is more persuasive than hate or indifference. We sense our passion's veracity for disclosing not only what is pleasing, but that which is holy.

Intentional communities and congregations are at their revealing best when the simplicity and beauty of their passion are sensed. The truth of their witness should be so obvious in their life together and mission that others are convinced of their integrity after accepting the invitation to "come and see." Radical discipleship occurs through the invitation to see the word made flesh. Passion embodied draws us and ignites our passion. Impassioned disciples experience the call to community to be a peculiar people in a particular place for an uncertain future. They are a people who live in covenantal fellowship with companions, being known and loved for better and for worse, for the glory of God.

Impassioned disciples create a holy order that clarifies the authority which maintains the boundaries of community, by trial and error and trial again. And they transform and are being transformed by prophetic neighboring that uses many means necessary to make all things new. The promise of God's promise to be with them is known when they respect common miracles, risk modest proposals, and are embraced by a love that defines and empowers them.

Intentional communities so easily magnify their members' passion. Their intensity also magnifies passion frustrated by the varying expectations and personal conflict within them—resulting in discord that debilitates and sometimes destroys. The fire that energizes can become the fire that consumes. Regardless, they at least give testimony to the reality and power of passion.

Members of congregations hunger to know if their fellowship is a place where their passion will be embraced, nourished, and released. In answering the call of God, they hunger to experience the very Heart of all passion. Every church has the choice to be such a place. Every church can be the crucible where radical discipleship is forged. This is the challenge and promise for the church today.

In the beginning is the image of God's promise. . . . In the image of God's promise is the beginning.

Notes

Chapter 1

1. "We Are One in the Spirit," words and music by Peter Scholtes (Los Angeles: F. E. L. Publications, 1966).

2. This caricature of the New Testament churches fails to recognize their susceptibility to err from Christlike principles. The Apostle Paul's letter to the church at Corinth provides some insight into early church problems.

3. *The Book of Discipline of the United Methodist Church: 1988* (Nashville: The United Methodist Publishing House, 1988), p. 94.

4. Perry Miller and Thomas H. Johnson, *The Puritans*, vol. I, rev. ed. (New York: Harper & Row, 1963), p. 181.

5. *Ibid.*, p. 199. To facilitate the reading of this text, the spelling of words in this quotation was changed to modern spelling standards.

6. See Charles Crowe, *George Ripley* (Athens, Ga.: University of Georgia Press, 1967), p. 69.

7. This interpretation does not apply to the situation of Native Americans and black slaves. The Native American increasingly lost land and freedom to settlers seeking to fulfill their "manifest destiny" by expanding into and subduing the wilderness. And the enslavement of black people was a process that intended to deny slaves any option of movement that might be even a tacit admission that slaves had rights.

8. Recognizing the important role of the frontier in American history, President John F. Kennedy used the frontier metaphor as the theme for his administrative thrust. He launched a variety of programs which promised to be the "New Frontier" for national resources and energies. Kennedy promised that the country's economic strength, moral resolve, and international influence would benefit from the adventure into the frontier.

9. Sydney E. Ahlstrom, *A Religious History of the American People* (New Haven: Yale University Press, 1972), p. 7.

10. The lay persons who lead these groups are not referred to as "leaders" by other community members. The terms "coordinator" or "facilitator" are used. This distinction is to move away from the notion of the people merely following the ideas and commitment of another. Coordination recognizes that the gifts of insight and understanding reside *within* the people. In this writing the term *leader* is used because it best communicates the role of these laypersons to audiences outside the BCC's context. However, it refers to one with accepted skills of guidance and organization rather than one with superior authority.

11. Philip Berryman, "Latin America: 'Iglesia que nace del pueblo,' " *Christianity and Crisis*, Vol. 41, No. 14 (Sept. 21, 1981), p. 239.

12. Harvey Cox, *Religion in the Secular City: Toward a Postmodern Theology* (New York: Simon and Schuster, 1984), p. 117.

13. For further insights on this critique, see Cornel West, "The North American Blacks," and James H. Cone, "From Geneva to Sao Paulo: A Dialogue Between Black Theology and Latin American Liberation Theology," in Sergio Torres and John Eagleson, eds., *The Challenge of Basic Christian Communities* (Maryknoll: Orbis, 1981), pp. 255-257 and pp. 265-281.

14. The phrase is taken from the community's brochure, *Koinonia Partners* (p. 5).

15. In building new homes for the poor, Koinonia has created a financing arrangement where the poor can buy the home under a no interest loan agreement that results in low monthly mortgage payments. In the 1970s the monthly payment was about $29 to $39. In 1990 the average monthly payment was $120. These payments remain considerably lower than what most poor families pay for rent.

16. From various sources, 180 communities were identified as having an interest in social issues. A questionnaire was mailed to these communities. Twenty-nine questionnaires were returned with the postal stamp "addressee unknown." Evidently these communities had terminated. Sixty-eight communities returned the questionnaire. The accuracy of these findings was checked by randomly selecting and surveying twenty-two of the remaining communities that had not responded to the questionnaire. The results of the larger survey were verified by this method. Every trend was found to be consistent in both surveys. This survey was conducted during the spring 1983.

Chapter 2

1. Dallas Lee, *The Cotton Patch Evidence: The Story of Clarence Jordan*

and the Koinonia Farm Experiment (1942 - 1970) (Americus, Ga.: Koinonia publications, 1971), p. 28.

2. *Ibid.*, p. 9.

3. Jim Wallis, *Revive Us Again: A Sojourner's Story* (Nashville: Abingdon, 1983), p. 94.

4. John Perkins, *With Justice for All* (Ventura, Calif.: Regal, 1982), p. 105.

5. *Atlanta Journal Constitution*, March 6, 1977.

6. Perkins, p. 106.

7. See W. Graham Pulkingham, *Gathered for Power: Charisma, Communalism, Christian Witness* (New York: Moorehouse-Barlow, 1973).

8. See Richard Quebedeaux, *The New Charismatics: The Origins, Development, and Significance of Neo-Pentecostalism* (Garden City, N.Y.: Doubleday, 1976), pp. 118-121.

9. Perkins, p. 109.

10. From a recorded lecture entitled "Metamorphosis."

11. "The Legacy of Clarence Jordan," interview by Walden Howard, *Faith at Work*, April 1970, p. 16.

12. Perkins, p. 20.

13. (Nashville: Abingdon, 1949), p. 7.

14. (Philadelphia: Fortress, 1977), pp. 3 and 6.

15. (New York: Meridian, 1929), p. 6.

16. See Luther E. Smith, Jr., "Christian Discipleship: Living Our Past and Future," *The People Called Methodist* (Nashville: Discipleship Resources, 1984), p. 54.

17. (Philadelphia and New York: Fortress and Paulist, 1984), pp. 75-147.

Chapter 3

1. In the survey of sixty-eight religious communities, one might consider the larger social climate to be an important "push factor" in their formation. These are relatively young religious fellowships. Eighty-seven percent of the communities began after 1965, and half have only been established since 1975. The 1970s was the boom decade for these communities. From 1971-79 we find that 63.3 percent of these communities were organized. None of the communities were begun between 1957-65; none of the twenty-two additional communities used to verify the survey data began during this period.

Such an obvious gap leads toward speculation about cultural trends that may have lessened interest in communalism. Considering the optimism which characterized much of the Eisenhower and Kennedy years, the availability of government programs (e.g., The Peace Corp and VIS-

TA) that attracted the imagination and dedication of youth for service, and the energy given to civil rights protests as activities of social transformation, perhaps these attitudes and opportunities were sufficient for those with a burning social concern.

But by the 1970s many were disillusioned with the government (especially because of its role in the Vietnam War and Watergate), its volunteer programs, and the effectiveness of the demonstrations for civil rights. Communal experiments then emerged as a viable option to address visionaries' social concern and personal quest for fulfillment.

2. Lee, p. 87.

3. In the survey of sixty-eight communities, most of the communities, regardless of membership size, had members live together in households. Of those communities with five members or less, all had the household living arrangement.

It is statistically significant that smaller communities (ten members or less) had a pooled economy or accepted voluntary poverty to a greater extent than communities with eleven or more members. [The term *significance* identifies those results that had a statistical probability <.05 (Chi-Square Test). Such a probability indicates an unusually strong correlation between the compared factors.] We find 71.4 percent of the communities with one–five members and 80 percent of the communities with six–ten members had this more structured economic arrangement. While among the larger communities only 47.4 percent of those with eleven-twenty members, only 36.4 percent of those with twenty-one to forty-five members, and only 44.4 percent of those with sixty-five members or more utilized the pooled or voluntary poverty economic arrangement.

There was no significant difference between Catholic communities and other communities in their economic and living arrangements nor in their mission aim.

4. Perhaps more than the other communities, Messiah accepted dealing with emotional crises as an essential act of its identity. This may be due to it being an Episcopal church obligated to welcome all, especially those in severe need. The institutional church has the ecclesiastical imperative to harbor all who seek refuge within the body of Christ. Historically this has even meant providing sanctuary to persons being persecuted by civil authority. Messiah's institutional heritage may bind it to accepting anyone who seeks the company of Christians. Unconditional acceptance supersedes restrictions on membership, even if goals of intentionality are hampered.

Messiah's institutional heritage, however, does not fully explain its openness. History also discloses that churches often fail to extend hospitality to those in need. Messiah has evidently drawn upon the more faithful expressions of its institutional heritage.

5. The metaphor "family" was especially used at Sojourners and Messiah, which still had common households late in their communal life. Members felt closely related to and responsible for one another in contexts of work and home. At Patchwork, VOC, and Koinonia, the sense of family existed as the feeling of being in covenant relationships that are bound by intimacy. But these communities did not embrace the implication of communal family as the definer and shaper of *home* life. Family was the operative metaphor at Koinonia early in its life when common households were the structured living arrangements.

6. Tape of Carlyle Marney's lecture "The Return of the Presence" (Lecture #2) at Furman University's 1971 Pastor's School (Atlanta: Protestant Radio and Television Center).

7. Howard Thurman, *Disciplines of the Spirit* (New York: Harper & Row, 1963), p. 35.

8. See Thomas E. Frank, "Practical Theology and the Study of Congregations," in *Landscape of the 90's: Tensions, Visions, Hope. Proceedings of the Association for Theological Field Education* (January 1991), pp. 52-57.

9. *A Catalogue of Sins: A Contemporary Examination of Christian Conscience* (New York: Holt, Rinehart and Winston, 1967), p. 197.

Chapter 4

1. Lee, pp. 69-70, and 177.

2. *Ibid.*, p. 84.

3. In 1993, the membership joining process required someone to begin as a program volunteer for three months. After that, the individual would become an extended volunteer for a maximum of two years. Within the first three months as an extended volunteer, the individual could petition the residency committee to become a novice, and therefore be on track to become a resident partner. This novice status usually lasted between three months to a year. The novice received a guide who helped in decisions about the commitment to partnership. Novices participated in all community activities, including the partners' meetings. When the novice and residency committee agreed that the novice was ready to become a resident partner, the novice would then assume the responsibilities of a resident partner.

4. In no sense do these communities perceive nonmembers as contaminators of their religious fellowship. The effort to govern relationships was strictly a matter of keeping *members* focused on commu-

nal commitments and covenant. It was never a statement about the virtue and worth of nonmembers.

By contrast, Rosabeth Moss Kanter, *Commitment and Community: Communes and Utopias in Sociological Perspective* (Cambridge: Harvard University Press, 1972), describes the rituals of the Oneida community that responded to the conviction that outsiders were contaminators. She writes, "Thus, after the daily visitors had left, those members most exposed to contact with them [outsiders] were required to submit to mutual criticism, so as to be 'freed from contamination by worldly influences.' Further, the whole group joined together for a ritualistic scrubbing 'bee,' to 'purify' the community" (p. 86). This attitude toward nonmembers considers them to be inferior persons who, by their very nature, threaten the well-being of the religious community.

5. In the larger survey of sixty-eight religious communities, the support group averaged twenty-one persons per community. The nonmember median in these communities was 14.5 [median indicates that an equal number of communities are below and above the given figure], which was only one person short of the member median of 15.5. Small communities had a group of supportive nonmembers that often exceeded the number of community members; 80 percent of the communities with five members or less had a support group which outnumbered the membership. Of the communities with six–ten members some 57 percent had a support group which exceeded membership numbers. Communities with eleven–twenty members had about as many members as supportive nonmembers. And communities with more than twenty-one members had a support group of eleven participants or more; the members were the majority among this numerical category. These figures suggest that the mere size of the support group makes it a critical factor in the dynamics of communalism.

6. Kanter, pp. 75-125.

7. Membership is essential to sustaining the existence and purpose of the community. Consequently, communities must be responsive to dissatisfaction that threatens to decrease membership to levels that threaten the viability of the community. Among the sixty-eight religious communities, 50 percent of them had fifteen or fewer members. A large number of these communities therefore operated as small groups. Eighty percent of the communities had thirty or fewer members. There was statistical significance between the size of a community and the number of years it has existed. There were no small communities (ten or fewer members) with a history of twelve years or more. Small communities tend to be short-lived.

When a small community of ten or fewer members lose five members, this represents at least half of the community. The impact on communal morale can be devastating. While a community of fifty will grieve the loss of five, the leave-taking is not as threatening to the viability of the fellowship. Membership retention, therefore, can be a life-or-death matter for small communities. Even if they want to remain small, they cannot afford to lose a small number of members (who may be a large percentage of the membership) without jeopardizing the vitality and existence of the fellowship.

    8. Avery Dulles, S.J., *Models of the Church* (Garden City, N.Y.: Doubleday & Company, 1974), p. 35.

Chapter 5

    1. *The VOC Story* (brochure of the Voice of Calvary Ministries).

    2. In the study of sixty-eight communities there are important insights regarding their location and ministries. About three-fourths of the communities had their facilities located in urban areas exclusively, 6 percent in towns, and 13 percent in open country. The rest indicated that their facilities were located in more than one type of setting.

    The economic status of the residents in the immediate area of these facilities was described as "lower" by 31.8 percent of the communities, and as "lower middle to low" by 19.7 percent. This means that a total of 51.5 percent of the communities had their facilities located in lower middle- and/or lower-class areas. Another 28.8 percent were in areas identified as "middle and low." This means a total of 80.3 percent of the communities had their facilities located in middle- and/or lower-class areas. Next, 13.6 percent of the communities were in areas identified solely as middle class. Some 4.5 percent of the communities had facilities in fully mixed (low, middle, and upper income) neighborhoods. Only 1.5 percent of the communities indicated that the residents in the area of their facilities were upper class. The racial composition of the area of their facilities was described as racially mixed by 60 percent of the communities, mostly white by 24 percent, mostly black by 12 percent, and Hispanic by 3 percent.

    A large percentage (83.9 percent) of the communities indicated that most of their membership lived in the area where their facilities were located. This means that most of these members lived in urban, lower-income, and racially mixed or minority areas. It is significant, however, that 100 percent of the communities in middle-income neighborhoods had most of their membership in the same area, yet only 78.7 percent of communities in economically low and mixed neighborhoods had most of their membership in such areas.

    While low-income neighborhoods were home for most community

members whose facilities were located there, communities located in middle-income areas were more likely to have their members reside in their immediate area.

3. Larry McAdoo, "Initiating Development Within the Community of Need," *A Quiet Revolution*, vol. 7, no. 4, Winter 1980-81, p. 7.

4. The extent to which the sixty-eight communities viewed the importance of social transformation can be garnered from their response to four statements about social change: 1.6 percent indicated that it (social change) is "no responsibility of the religious community, since if individuals are soundly converted, social problems will take care of themselves"; 9.8 percent marked that it is "a partial responsibility of religious communities but secondary to the transformation of individuals"; 75.4 percent affirmed social change to be "of equal importance with individual transformation"; and 13.1 percent indicated that it "is even more important than individual conversion, since social conditions greatly affect individuals." Their outreach was not just an evangelistic tool to convert the people they served, but outreach had integrity as a vital expression of Christian faith.

These communities' major goals and purposes, listed in order that was most checked, were to build a new society, nurture personal development and spiritual renewal, build a nurturing community, simplify lives, praise and worship God, and to meet members' and neighbors' needs.

Among the issues listed by these communities were (the numbers indicate the percentage of the communities that identified the issue as a concern): peace issues such as opposing military buildup and pro nuclear freeze (80.9 percent); poor and homeless (52.9 percent); women's issues (29.4 percent); international politics (20.6 percent); criminal justice (17.6 percent); opposing abortion (16.2 percent); youth concerns (14.7 percent). Concerns that were identified by 10 percent or less of the communities were: assisting refugees, elderly, mentally and physically handicapped, and conservation.

The various forms of involvement listed by the communities were providing service (76.5 percent); demonstrations (73.5 percent); work with agencies (44.1 percent); political activity (41.2 percent); neighborhood organizing (38.2 percent); educational (27.9 percent); creating business (7.4 percent). When asked about unacceptable methods of social change the communities listed: violence (94.1 percent); politics (8.8 percent); partisan politics (5.9 percent); participation with government agencies (1.5 percent); and civil disobedience (1.5 percent).

Statistical significance does occur when the location of a community's facilities is cross-tabulated with the identification of the "inner city" or "poor" as the particular area upon which mission is focused. No community with facilities in a "mostly white" area identified the inner city as the focus of its mission. Yet, 37.5 percent of the communities in mostly black neighborhoods and 20.5 percent of the communities in racially mixed neighborhoods identified the inner city as a particular area for mission. No community whose mission was particularly focused upon a poor area had its facilities located in a middle-income neighborhood; all communities with such a focus were located in low and economically mixed neighborhoods.

There is also statistical significance between the racial character of the neighborhood in which a community's facilities were located and its identification of the poor as a particular group upon which social change activities were directed. The poor were a particular group for only 6.3 percent of the communities in mostly white neighborhoods, but were a particular group for 37.5 percent of those communities in mostly black neighborhoods and 56.4 percent of those in racially mixed neighborhoods. One might ask if being located in neighborhoods with black residents leads to concern for the poor, or if concern for the poor leads one to locate in neighborhoods with black residents. Either way, this is a rather important correlation about location and mission.

5. *Stitches*, vol. 14, no. 1, February 1990, p. 2.

6. The sixty-eight religious communities of the survey tended not to have much diversity. Almost 60 percent of the communities were all white in their membership. And 80 percent of the communities had a membership which was 90 percent white. Only thirteen communities had black members; among these thirteen, black members averaged 6.3 percent of total membership. Only ten communities had Hispanic members, and they averaged 17.6 percent of these communities' total membership. Five communities had Asian-Americans and three communities had Native Americans.

About 66 percent of the membership of these communities was in the twenty-one to forty-five age-group. This age-group was only 38.6 percent of the U.S. population. Least attracted to these communities were the elderly. Among the communities persons sixty-five years of age and older averaged only 1.65 percent of their membership, while this age-group was 11.6 percent of the U.S. population.

The disparity in elderly members was even greater when compared to the membership of some denominations. Those fifty-five years of age and older were 6.5 percent of the membership of these communities; while in the United Methodist Church this age-group was 43 percent of the church's membership, and 39 percent of the membership of the United Presbyterian Church.

The age statistics might be explained by communalism's high demand upon time and energy. Communal mission endeavors and the various living and economic arrangements are geared for persons with a spirit of experimentation and with considerable energy. Certainly there are many elderly full of vigor and openness to new experiences. Some religious communities specialize in having older members. The majority of this society's elderly, however, might find the pace of communal life strenuous and unstable.

The thirteen–twenty age-group averaged 16.6 percent of the communities' membership. About 80 percent of the communities had 10 percent or less of their membership in this age-group, and 67 percent of the communities had no membership in this grouping. Such statistics could be explained by the age of the communities; the young people who joined were not members long enough for their children to become adolescents. However, the community life itself might explain the low number of adolescents; that is, the expectations and demands of living in community were very difficult for adolescents and their parents to endure.

The communities had about an even number of males and females. There were more single persons (averaging 60.5 percent) in the communities.

These figures do not necessarily indicate that religious communalism is exclusive. One can find communities in the U.S. that have a majority of black persons (Voice of Calvary) or elderly persons (Koinonia Partners). The statistics do, however, indicate a membership profile that suggests intentional communities primarily attract younger, white, and probably middle-class persons. The support groups of these communities probably bring diversity to their fellowship which is lacking in their membership.

7. (New York: Vintage, 1961).

8. *Mysticism and the Experience of Love* (Wallingford, Pa.: Pendle Hill, 1961), p. 15.

9. (New York: Vintage, 1963), p. 476.

Chapter 6

1. "Getting It all Together: Group Issues in Contemporary Communes," *Communes: Creating and Managing the Collective Life* (New York: Harper & Row, 1973), p. 407.

2. Helen Bruch Pearson, *Do What You Have the Power to Do: Studies of Six New Testament Women* (Nashville: Upper Room Books, 1992) examines how women, though hindered by oppressive social and religious customs, were able to bear witness to God's liberating and trans-

forming power. Her excellent study indicates how women, in their encounter with Jesus, had every reason to retreat from the challenge created by faith confronting crisis. Instead, they refused to be imprisoned by their circumstances; they found a way to make use of limited abilities that not only changed their lives, but also changed Jesus' life and our lives.

3. William Bailey Williford, *Americus Through the Years: The Story of A Georgia Town and Its People, 1832-1975* (Atlanta: Cherokee Publishing, 1975), pp. 337-338.

4. *Mysticism* (New York: Meridian, 1955), p. 258.

The Author

Luther E. Smith, Jr., is associate professor of church and community at The Candler School of Theology of Emory University, Atlanta, Georgia. He holds a Ph.D. in American studies from St. Louis University.

Dr. Smith has written numerous articles and speaks extensively on issues of church and society, congregational renewal, Christian spirituality, and the thought of Howard Thurman. He is the author of *Howard Thurman: The Mystic and Prophet* (Friends United Press, 1991) and editor of *The Pan Methodist Social Witness Resource Book* (A.M.E. Publishing House, 1991).

Luther Smith is an ordained minister of the Christian Methodist Episcopal Church. He is active in religious and civic organizations, especially ecumenical efforts to address social concerns. He is a certified mediator for court cases requiring conflict resolution. Congregations and ecumenical groups often call on him as a consultant for their initiatives in social ministry.